200
FAMILY SLOW COOKER RECIPES

D0718766

200
FAMILY SLOW
COOKER RECIPES

SARA LEWIS

First published in Great Britain in 2016 by
Hamlyn, a division of Octopus Publishing Group Ltd
Carmelite House, 50 Victoria Embankment,
London EC4Y 0DZ
www.octopusbooks.co.uk

An Hachette UK Company
www.hachette.co.uk

Some of this material previously appeared in other books
published by Hamlyn.

Copyright © Octopus Publishing Group Ltd 2016

All rights reserved. No part of this work may be reproduced
or utilized in any form or by any means, electronic or
mechanical, including photocopying, recording or by any
information storage and retrieval system, without the prior
written permission of the publisher.

Sara Lewis asserts the moral right to be identified as the
author of this work.

ISBN 978-0-600-63057-9

A CIP catalogue record for this book is available from the
British Library.

Printed and bound in China.

11

Standard level spoon measurement are used in all recipes.
1 tablespoon = one 15 ml spoon
1 teaspoon = one 5 ml spoon

Both imperial and metric measures have been given in
all recipes. Use one set of measurements only and not a
mixture of both.

Eggs should be medium unless otherwise stated. The
Department of Health advises that eggs should not be
consumed raw. This book contains dishes made with raw
or lightly cooked eggs. It is prudent for more vulnerable
people such as pregnant and nursing mothers, invalids,
the elderly, babies and young children to avoid uncooked
or lightly cooked dishes made with eggs. Once prepared
these dishes should be kept refrigerated and used promptly.

Ovens should be preheated to the specific temperature
– if using a fan-assisted oven, follow the manufacturer's
instructions for adjusting the time and the temperature.

This book includes dishes made with nuts and nut
derivatives. It is advisable for customers with known allergic
reactions to nuts and nut derivatives and those who may be
potentially vulnerable to these allergies, such as pregnant
and nursing mothers, invalids, the elderly, babies and
children, to avoid dishes made with nuts and nut oils. It is
also prudent to check the labels of pre-prepared ingredients
for the possible inclusion of nut derivatives.

contents

introduction

introduction

Slow cooking is fashionable again and what easier way is there to make a meal than in a slow cooker? It's cheaper than turning on the oven, as it uses much less electricity, and a slow cooker is compact, too.

As food cooks gradually and gently, veggies become wonderfully flavourful and meat becomes meltingly tender, which means that cheaper cuts of meat can be given the five-star treatment in a slow cooker. Make the most of special offers and make double the quantity, so that half can be frozen for another meal. Or make smaller amounts of meat go further by combining them with healthy root and Mediterranean vegetables, pulses, grains and lentils.

But a slow cooker isn't just for casseroles and stews, great though they are. You can make a huge variety of other dishes with this gadget, including lighter meals, delicious fish recipes and child-pleasing suppers. Try warming main meal soups such as Pumpkin, Carrot & Quinoa (see page 22) or Country Mushroom & Bacon (see page 38); kids' favourites such as Tuna Pasta Bake (see page 48) and Chicken & Mango Curry (see page 54); everyday favourites such as White Bean & Chipotle Chilli (see page 80) and Piri Piri Chicken (see page 92); easy cheats such as Red Pepper & Chorizo Tortilla (see page 120) and Thai Beef Curry (see page 138), and food to impress such as Seafood Laksa (see page 150) and Rioja-braised Lamb with Olives (see page 170). To finish things off, nostalgic puds like Sticky Toffee Pudding (see page 188) and Plum & Blueberry Betty (see page 186) can become home-cooked treats once more with a slow cooker.

If you're unfamiliar with using a slow cooker, the redistribution of time involved may seem odd. Early on in the day, you spend 15 minutes in the kitchen doing a little prep, then add everything to the slow cooker, and you can walk away and get on with something else. While cooking before you rush out to work in the morning may not be for everyone, getting a lovely supper on to cook before you head out to the golf course, for a day of shopping with a girlfriend or before doing the Saturday taxi run to and from the kids' clubs may seem more manageable.

As the slow cooker cooks so gently, there's no need to stir or check on the food because there is no danger of it drying out or spoiling. Just enjoy the welcoming aroma of a delicious supper ready and waiting when you walk back through the door.

New to slow cooking? Your questions answered

Are all slow cookers the same?

All slow cookers cook food slowly, though they do vary slightly. Oval-shaped slow cookers offer the most flexibility when it comes to cooking joints or desserts. Generally, slow cookers come in three sizes:

- a two-portion size with a capacity of 1.5 litres (2½ pints)
- a four-portion size with a capacity of 2.5 litres (4 pints)
- a six-to-eight portion size with a capacity of 4 litres (7 pints) or 4.5 litres (8 pints).

Newer models might come with cooking pots that can be used on the hob, so you can fry off meat and onions prior to slow cooking in the slow cooker pot itself, saving on washing up. These types of slow cookers do tend to cost more. A good nonstick frying pan in conjunction with a slow cooker works just as well.

As with all things, price varies considerably. The larger models are very often on special offer, but unless your family is large or you plan to cook larger quantities in order to

freeze half of the batch, you may find that, while the machine itself is a good price, you have to cook larger quantities than you had expected in order to just half-fill it.

When selecting a slow cooker, choose a machine with a high and low setting and an on/off light at the front of the machine so that you can see easily that it is on. There is nothing more frustrating than to come back eight hours later, expecting a hot, delicious meal, only to find that you haven't turned the machine on! Some models have a setting that allows you to keep the food warm, which is useful. Digital clocks are great, but they are certainly not essential.

Dull though it sounds, once you've purchased a slow cooker, make sure you read the handbook. The majority of models should *not* be preheated with an empty slow cooker pot. If you part-prep supper the night before and put the earthenware slow cooker pot in the refrigerator, all manufacturers agree that you should leave it at room temperature for 20 minutes before adding it to the slow cooker machine and turning it on.

Is it safe to leave it on all day?

Yes – the slow cooker runs on such a small amount of power (the equivalent of two light bulbs) that it is safe to leave it on all day – even if you go out. Because the heat is so low and the lid forms a seal, there is no danger of the food boiling dry. The sides of the slow cooker will feel warm to the touch, so ensure you leave the machine on a non-cluttered part of the work surface.

Do I have to fry foods before I add them to the slow cooker pot?

Frying onions and browning meat adds colour and flavour to the finished casserole, but it isn't essential – it's very much a matter of personal taste. Foods will not brown in a slow cooker. The idea of frying before you rush out in the morning can be a bit off-putting, especially if are wearing your smart work clothes, so there are plenty of recipes in the book that can be made without precooking. Boost colour and flavour with tomato purée, red wine or beer, spices or herbs, and away you go. But if you have a young family, it can be great to come back from the morning school or nursery drop-off and to get supper on while the house is quieter.

Does liquid have to be hot before going in the slow cooker?

The slow cooker works by building up heat to just below boiling point, then safely maintaining the heat so that food cooks gently but without any danger of allowing the bacteria that cause food poisoning to proliferate. If you add all cold ingredients, this will obviously extend the heating-up process, so add 2–3 hours to the cooking time, with the first hour on high, especially if the recipe states to use hot stock. But it is much quicker and very simple to dissolve a stock cube in boiling water and add the hot stock to the slow cooker pot. Always add hot liquid when cooking large joints.

How full should the pot be?

Ideally, the slow cooker pot should be filled half full and up to three-quarters full for it to work efficiently. For soups, fill it so that the liquid is 5 cm (2 inches) from the top. If you have a very large slow cooker, make up amounts to serve six to eight people, then freeze the extra in single portions or portion sizes that will suit your family on another day. As the slow cooker heats up, the steam generated will condense and make a water seal between the lid and top of the slow cooker pot – this is perfectly normal.

Can I use my ordinary recipes?

Yes, of course – stews, casseroles and pot roast recipes can all be made in the slow cooker with the same ingredients. However, because the slow cooker creates a seal during cooking, the liquid doesn't evaporate, so you'll find you need to reduce the liquid in your recipes by one third, and sometimes even by half. For stews or casseroles just cover the meat or vegetables with stock. Bear in mind, if using fresh tomatoes, that you will need slightly less stock as the tomatoes will pulp down as they cook.

Depending on the size of your slow cooker pot you may need to cut down or size up the quantities of ingredients given in the recipes. A medium-sized slow cooker pot comfortably makes four portions, while a large one makes six to eight portions. Many of the recipes in this book are designed to feed four people – ideal for a medium-sized slow pot.

The slow cooker can also be used as a bain-marie or steamer. Making steamed puddings works very well and you don't need to top up with boiling water during cooking as there's no chance the water will boil dry.

As a rough guide, if a recipe takes 1–2 hours on the hob or in the oven you should cook it in a slow cooker for 3–4 hours on the high setting, or 6–8 hours on the low setting. If a recipe takes 2–4 hours on the hob or in the oven, cook it in the slow cooker for 4–6 hours on high, or for 8–12 hours on low.

Can I cook rice and pasta?

Yes, but as they are both starchy foods they can go sticky and gluey if overcooked. Choose easy-cook rice over ordinary rice where available, as some of the starch has been removed during manufacturing, making it less sticky. If making a risotto, add the stock all in one go rather than a ladleful at a time.

Cook pasta in a saucepan of boiling water, then drain and stir it into the slow cooker pot

just before serving. For lasagne, use 'no pre-cooking' dried lasagne sheets and cook for no more than 5–6¼ hours. Tiny pasta shapes can be added to soups, without cooking first, for the final 15–30 minutes of cooking time.

What about dairy foods and shellfish?

Dairy foods, such as milk, double cream and grated Cheddar-style cheeses, are fine for recipes with short cooking times, or in baked dishes that are cooked for up to 3–5 hours on a low setting, or can be stirred into a dish towards the end of cooking so that they have the final 15–30 minutes to add richness and flavour. If you cook them too long they will separate rather unattractively.

Shellfish can be added to a dish, but in small quantities only and, again, towards the end of the cooking time, when the other ingredients are already piping hot. Make sure that the shellfish is also piping hot before

serving, so cook it on high, preferably for 15 minutes, then serve. Do not keep dishes containing shellfish warm. If you are using frozen fish, ensure that it is fully defrosted before adding it to the slow cooker pot.

Can I reheat foods in the slow cooker?

All manufacturers recommend that you only cook foods from raw in the slow cooker pot. To reheat a casserole or stew, put it in a saucepan, set it on the hob and bring it up to the boil, stirring, then cook for at least 10 minutes until thoroughly reheated and piping hot throughout. Only reheat cooked food once.

remember the basics

- Always add liquid to a slow cooker pot, ideally hot or boiling water.
- Test food before serving it to ensure it is thoroughly cooked before serving. Chicken or pork should have no pink juices when they are pierced with a small, sharp knife. Beef and lamb should be tender. Fish should flake into even-coloured flakes when pressed with a knife.
- Remove the slow cooker pot from the machine when the dish is cooked using oven gloves to serve.
- Cover any remaining food, allow it to cool, then transfer it to the refrigerator as soon as possible.

- If using raw frozen food other than peas or sweetcorn, defrost before use.
- Do not reheat food in a slow cooker (Christmas pudding is the exception).

Getting the most from your slow cooker

Get ahead

Just 15 minutes' prep is all it takes to get a good meal underway, but trying to do that before you go out to work in the mornings might be a tall order. To make mornings easier, you could prepare meat and vegetables the night before – peeling onions and chopping meat and storing them in the refrigerator in plastic containers, for instance. Marinating foods overnight adds flavour, helps to tenderize meat and saves time next day – you could fry them or add them straight to the slow cooker pot in the morning with hot stock. Cover, set the temperature and walk away.

Short of time?

Not all slow cooker recipes need 8–10 hours to cook. There are plenty that can be served in 5–6 hours that you can put on after dropping the kids to school, so the meal will be ready by pick-up time. If shorter cooking times appeal to you, as a quick guide, look for recipes in this book that use a small joint or that are cooked on the high setting. Or if you just have two hours and need a lunch to share with a friend, choose a risotto or a gently cooked fish dish.

Combining meat and vegetables

Nutritionists and dieticians all recommend that we cut down on the amount of meat we eat. Adding vegetables, canned pulses and dried lentils to an everyday meaty casserole not only adds essential fibre, vitamins and minerals, but also helps to reduce the meat content of the recipe – which makes it cheaper, too. For fussy eaters, grate or very finely chop veggies so that they go unnoticed.

Surprisingly, diced root vegetables take as long to cook as meat – and even longer, if they are cut into large chunks. Cut all the root veggies the same size and, if anything, slightly smaller than the size of the meaty pieces so that they will all be cooked at the same time, and press beneath the liquid level so that they cook evenly.

There's no need to cook crunchy green veg like broccoli, spinach and kale separately – just cut them into small pieces and add them to the slow cooker for the final 15–30 minutes of cooking so they stay bright green.

it won't stick or boil dry as it cooks. Don't be tempted to lift open the lid – every time you do so you release some of the heat and can add up to 10–15 minutes to the cooking time. It's much better to peer through the glass lid, and stir just once before serving or when adding extra ingredients towards the end of the cooking time.

Thickening

As the liquid in a recipe doesn't reduce down during slow cooking, you may like to add a little thickening agent to the sauce. This can be done either after frying, by sprinkling in a little plain flour to fried onions and meat, or at the end of the cooking time, by stirring in a teaspoonful or two of cornflour mixed to a paste with water for the final 15 minutes of cooking. For pot roasts, you can strain off or ladle out the liquid at the end of cooking and reduce it by boiling it rapidly in a saucepan for 10 minutes.

Double up

If your family is small, cook the maximum amount that you can in your slow cooker, take out enough for your supper, then cool the remainder and freeze it in handy-sized packs, ready for those days when you don't have time to cook, or the kids need something you can microwave when you are home late.

You can use frozen veggies, such as peas or sweetcorn, in a dish – they don't need to be defrosted first. Just add them in small amounts, so that they don't cool down the liquid too much, for the final 15–30 minutes of the cooking time. Upping the amount of vegetables helps to keep calories low. To cut calories even more, trim off the fat or skin from meat and poultry before cooking.

Combined temperatures

Most of the stews and casseroles in the book are cooked on low, but it can be helpful to raise the temperature to high for the final 15–60 minutes of cooking time, especially if adding extra vegetables, prawns, dumplings or cobbler toppings, or other finishing touches.

Don't be tempted to peek

As a slow cooker cooks so gently, there really is no need for you to stir the food because

Tips

- As foods cook so slowly in a slow cooker you can make use of cheaper beef cuts – such as blade, skirt, cheek or oxtail – without compromising on flavour. Don't forget neck of lamb on the bone or lamb breast, too. And bear in mind that chicken thighs taste better in the slow cooker than the more expensive chicken breasts!

- Foods will not brown in the slow cooker, so add colour to your stews by frying onions and meats first, adding spices or herbs, tomatoes or tomato purée, wine or beer, gravy browning or even Marmite (yeast extract).

- Save on washing up by puréeing soups while they are still in the slow cooker pot using a hand-held electric stick blender.

- Getting a steamed pudding out of the slow cooker pot can be tricky, especially if the basin is quite a snug fit in the pot. Tie string around the basin to make a handle to use to lift the pudding dish out of the slow cooker pot. Alternatively, fold two pieces of foil individually to make two long straps. Form a cross with the straps and place them on the work surface, then place the pudding dish on the cross and use the lengths of foil to lift up and lower the dish into the slow cooker pot. Tuck the straps over the top of the basin, then use them to lift out the pudding dish at the end of the cooking time.

- Food at the bottom of the slow cooker pot will cook more quickly than the rest, so add diced potatoes to the pot first, as these can take longer to cook than meat. Or, if you are adding lots of root veggies, cut them into chunks the same size or slightly smaller than the meat you are using and mix up the meat and veggie chunks.

- Short of time? Then cheat! Add a jar or can of ready-made sauce instead of making your own.

main meal
soups

spicy tomato & bean soup

Preparation time **15 minutes**
Cooking temperature **low**
Cooking time **8–9 hours**
Serves **4**

1 tablespoon **olive oil**
1 **onion**, chopped
2 **garlic cloves**, finely chopped
½ teaspoon **hot smoked paprika** or **chilli powder**
300 ml (½ pint) **vegetable stock**
2 teaspoons **light muscovado sugar**
½ teaspoon **dried oregano**
1 tablespoon **tomato purée**
625 g (1¼ lb) **tomatoes**, skinned if liked, cut into chunks
400 g (13 oz) can **cannellini beans**, drained
salt and **pepper**
warm **garlic bread**, to serve

Preheat the slow cooker if necessary; see the manufacturer's instructions. Heat the oil in a frying pan, add the onion and fry over a medium heat for 4–5 minutes, stirring, until the onion is lightly browned. Stir in the garlic and paprika or chilli powder.

Pour in the stock, add the sugar, oregano and tomato purée. Season with salt and pepper and bring to the boil, stirring.

Add the tomatoes and cannellini beans to the slow cooker pot, then pour in the stock mixture. Stir everything together, then cover and cook on low for 8–9 hours until the vegetables are tender.

Taste and adjust the seasoning, if needed. Ladle into bowls and serve with warm garlic bread.

For spicy tomato & chorizo soup, make up the soup as above, omitting the canned beans and adding 300 g (10 oz) diced potato and 100 g (3½ oz) diced chorizo sausage to the slow cooker pot before pouring in the stock mixture. Cook and serve as above.

cauliflower, leek & stilton soup

Preparation time **25 minutes**
Cooking temperature **high**
Cooking time **3¾–5 hours**
Serves **4**

1 tablespoon **olive oil**
25 g (1 oz) **butter**
1 large **leek**, chopped
2 tablespoons **long-grain white rice**
900 ml (1½ pints) **vegetable stock**
1 **cauliflower**, cut into florets
450 ml (¾ pint) **semi-skimmed milk**
125 g (4 oz) **Stilton** or other **blue cheese**, rind removed, cheese crumbled
6 rashers **smoked streaky bacon**, grilled until crispy, to garnish (optional)
salt and **pepper**

Preheat the slow cooker if necessary; see the manufacturer's instructions. Heat the oil and butter in a saucepan, add the leek and fry gently for 3–4 minutes until softened. Add the rice and stock, season with salt and pepper and bring to the boil, stirring.

Add the cauliflower to the slow cooker pot, pour over the hot stock mixture, cover with the lid and cook on high for 3–4 hours or until the cauliflower is tender.

Purée the soup while still in the slow cooker pot using a stick blender, or transfer to a blender, blend, then pour back into the slow cooker pot. Stir in the cold milk, then re-cover and cook for 45–60 minutes until piping hot. Stir in half the cheese, then ladle into bowls. Sprinkle with the remaining cheese and garnish with chopped grilled crispy bacon, if liked. Sprinkle with some freshly ground black pepper and serve with warm crusty bread, if liked.

For cauliflower, leek & watercress soup, make up the soup as above, adding just 300 ml (½ pint) milk. Omit the Stilton or blue cheese and add 50 g (2 oz) finely chopped watercress, 150 ml (¼ pint) double cream and 1–2 teaspoons Dijon mustard (to taste) to the puréed soup. Re-cover and cook in the slow cooker for 30–45 minutes. Serve topped with diced grilled bacon.

pumpkin, carrot & quinoa soup

Preparation time **25 minutes**
Cooking temperature **low**
Cooking time **7–8 hours**
Serves **4**

1 tablespoon **olive oil**
1 **onion**, chopped
1.2 litres (2 pints) **vegetable stock**
2 teaspoons **harissa paste**, plus extra to serve
500 g (1 lb) **ready-prepared pumpkin** or **butternut squash**, cut into 2 cm (¾ inch) dice
2 **carrots**, diced
40 g (1½ oz) **quinoa**
salt and **pepper**
handful of **coriander**, roughly chopped, to garnish

Preheat the slow cooker if necessary; see the manufacturer's instructions. Heat the oil in a saucepan, add the onion and fry for 4–5 minutes, stirring, until softened. Pour in the vegetable stock and add the harissa, season with salt and pepper and bring to the boil, stirring.

Add the pumpkin or squash, carrots and quinoa to the slow cooker pot, pour over the hot stock mixture, then cover with the lid and cook on low for 7–8 hours or until the vegetables are tender.

Mash the hot soup. Taste and adjust the seasoning, if needed. Ladle into bowls, top with a little extra harissa and sprinkle with chopped coriander.

For carrot & rice soup, add 625 g (1¼ lb) diced carrots to the slow cooker pot instead of the mixture of pumpkin and carrots, with 40 g (1½ oz) white long-grain rice instead of the quinoa. Add 1 teaspoon curry powder and 2 finely chopped garlic cloves to the hot stock mix instead of the harissa. Cook and serve as above.

beetroot & apple soup

Preparation time **25 minutes**
Cooking temperature **low**
Cooking time **8–9 hours**
Serves **4–6**

1 tablespoon **olive oil**
1 **onion**, chopped
1 litre (1¾ pints) **vegetable stock**
400 g (13 oz) trimmed **raw beetroot**, peeled and cut into 2 cm (¾ inch) cubes
1 **cooking apple**, about 250 g (8 oz), peeled, cored and diced
salt and **pepper**

Fennel & chilli croûtes
75 g (3 oz) **butter**, at room temperature
1 teaspoon **fennel seeds**, roughly crushed
¼ teaspoon **crushed dried red chillies**
3 tablespoons chopped **parsley** or **chives**
1 small **baguette**, thickly sliced

Preheat the slow cooker if necessary; see the manufacturer's instructions. Heat the oil in a saucepan, add the onion and fry for 5 minutes, stirring, until softened. Add the stock, season with salt and pepper and bring to the boil, stirring.

Add the beetroot and apple to the slow cooker pot. Pour over the hot stock mixture. Cover and cook on low for 8–9 hours or until the beetroot is tender.

Meanwhile, mix the butter with the fennel seeds, chillies and chopped herbs. Put the mixture into a small dish, cover and chill until needed.

Purée the soup using a stick blender in the slow cooker pot, or transfer the mixture to a blender and purée, then pour it back into the slow cooker pot. Taste and adjust the seasoning, if needed. Grill the bread on both sides, then spread with the flavoured butter. Ladle the hot soup into bowls and float the croûtes on top. Serve immediately.

For beetroot & carrot soup with herb croûtes, omit the cooking apple and add 250 g (8 oz) diced carrot. Cook as above. For the croûtes, mix 75 g (3 oz) butter with 3 tablespoons mixed fresh chopped herbs only, then spread the flavoured butter over the sliced grilled baguette as above.

vegetable broth with dumplings

Preparation time **35 minutes**
Cooking temperature **low**
Cooking time **8¾–11 hours**
Serves **4**

40 g (1½ oz) **butter**
1 **leek**, sliced, white and green
  parts kept separate
150 g (5 oz) **swede**, diced
150 g (5 oz) **parsnips**, diced
150 g (5 oz) **carrots**, diced
1 **celery stick**, sliced
50 g (2 oz) **pearl barley**
1 litre (1¾ pints) **boiling
  vegetable** or **chicken stock**
2–3 **sage sprigs**
1 teaspoon **English mustard**
salt and **pepper**

Dumplings
75 g (3 oz) **self-raising flour**
40 g (1½ oz) **vegetable suet**
2 **streaky bacon rashers**,
  finely diced
about 3 tablespoons **water**

Preheat the slow cooker if necessary; see the manufacturer's instructions. Heat the butter in a large frying pan, add the white leek slices, reserving the green slices and fry for 2–3 minutes until softened. Stir in the root vegetables and celery and fry for 4–5 minutes.

Add the pearl barley to the slow cooker pot, then add the fried vegetables, boiling stock and sage. Stir in the mustard and a little salt and pepper. Cover with the lid and cook on low for 8–10 hours or until the vegetables and barley are tender.

Make the dumplings. Put the flour, suet, bacon and a little salt and pepper into a bowl and mix well. Gradually stir in enough of the measurement water to make a soft but not sticky dough. Knead lightly on a floured surface, then shape into 12 balls.

Stir the reserved green leek slices into the soup, add the dumplings, spacing them slightly apart, then re-cover and continue to cook for 45–60 minutes or until light and fluffy. Ladle into bowls and serve.

For chicken broth with mini herb dumplings, fry 4 small chicken thighs on the bone with the white leek slices. Add the root vegetables and celery, omitting the parsnips. Continue and cook as above for 8–10 hours. Make the dumplings with 2 tablespoons mixed chopped parsley or chives and sage instead of the bacon. Lift the chicken out of the soup, discard the skin and bones and chop the meat into small pieces. Return the meat to the pot with the raw dumplings and green leeks, re-cover and cook for 45–60 minutes.

spiced parsnip & red lentil soup

Preparation time **25 minutes**
Cooking temperature **low**
Cooking time **7–8 hours**
Serves **4**

25 g (1 oz) **butter**
1 tablespoon **olive oil**
1 **onion**, chopped
1 **garlic clove**, finely chopped
1 teaspoon **ground coriander**
½ teaspoon **ground cumin**
½ teaspoon **turmeric**
1 litre (1¾ pints) **vegetable stock**
500 g (1 lb) **parsnips**, cut into chunks
50 g (2 oz) **red lentils**
salt and **pepper**

To serve
125 ml (4 fl oz) **double cream**
2 tablespoons **sweet chilli sauce**

Preheat the slow cooker if necessary; see the manufacturer's instructions. Heat the butter and oil in a saucepan, add the onion and fry for 5 minutes, stirring, until softened. Stir in the garlic and spices, then mix in the stock. Add a little salt and pepper and bring to the boil, stirring.

Add the parsnips and red lentils to the slow cooker pot. Pour over the hot stock mixture, then cover with the lid and cook on low for 7–8 hours until the parsnips and lentils are tender.

Purée with a stick blender in the slow cooker pot or transfer to a blender, blend, then return the mixture to the slow cooker pot. Taste and adjust the seasoning, if needed. Ladle into bowls, drizzle the cream and chilli sauce over and serve immediately.

For gingered sweet potato & red lentil soup, fry the onion in the butter as above, stir in the spices, then add a 4 cm (1½ inch) piece of peeled and finely chopped fresh root ginger with the garlic. Add 500 g (1 lb) peeled sweet potatoes, cut into chunks, in place of the parsnips to the slow cooker pot with the lentils. Add the remaining ingredients and cook as above. Purée with a handful of coriander leaves and serve with just a swirl of cream.

garlicky aubergine & spinach soup

Preparation time **20 minutes**
Cooking temperature **high**
  and **low**
Cooking time **5¼–6¼ hours**
Serves **4**

2 tablespoons **olive oil**
1 **onion**, finely chopped
1 **aubergine**, cut into small
  cubes
200 g (7 oz) **potato**, cut into
  small cubes
2 **garlic cloves**, finely chopped
1 teaspoon **ground cumin**
1 teaspoon **ground coriander**
100 g (3½ oz) **green lentils**
juice of 1 **lemon**
1 litre (1¾ pints) **boiling
  vegetable stock**
125 g (4 oz) **young spinach
  leaves**, larger leaves torn
  into pieces
salt and **pepper**

Preheat the slow cooker if necessary; see the manufacturer's instructions. Heat the oil in a large frying pan, add the onion and aubergine and fry for 5 minutes, stirring, until softened and lightly browned.

Stir in the potato, garlic and ground spices, then tip into the slow cooker pot. Add the lentils and lemon juice, then pour in the hot stock. Season with a little salt and pepper, then cover with the lid and cook on high for 5–6 hours or until the lentils are tender.

Add the spinach leaves, pressing them beneath the liquid, re-cover the slow cooker and cook on low for 15 minutes, until the spinach has just wilted and is still bright green in colour. Taste and adjust the seasoning, if needed. Ladle into bowls and serve with warm crusty bread, if liked.

For curried aubergine & spinach soup, fry the onion and aubergine as above. Add the potato, garlic and 4 teaspoons mild curry paste or powder instead of the ground spices. Add the lentils, a 400 g (13 oz) can chopped tomatoes and just 600 ml (1 pint) boiling vegetable stock. Omit the lemon juice and cook as above, adding the spinach for the last 15 minutes of cooking, as above.

salmon in hot miso broth

Preparation time **20 minutes**
Cooking temperature **low**
 and **high**
Cooking time **1 hour**
 40 minutes—2 hours
 10 minutes
Serves **6**

4 **salmon steaks**, about
 125 g (4 oz) each
1 **carrot**, thinly sliced
4 **spring onions**, thinly sliced
4 **cup mushrooms**, about
 125 g (4 oz) in total,
 thinly sliced
1 large **red chilli,** halved,
 deseeded and finely
 chopped
2 cm (¾ inch) **piece of fresh
 root ginger,** peeled and
 finely chopped
3 tablespoons **miso**
1 tablespoon **dark soy sauce**
2 tablespoons **mirin** (optional)
1.2 litres (2 pints) **boiling
 fish stock**
75 g (3 oz) **mangetout**,
 thinly sliced
coriander leaves, to garnish

Preheat the slow cooker if necessary; see the manufacturer's instructions. Rinse the salmon in cold water, drain and place in the slow cooker pot. Arrange the carrot, spring onions, mushrooms, chilli and ginger on top of the fish.

Add the miso, soy sauce and mirin, if using, to the boiling stock and stir until the miso has dissolved. Pour the stock mixture over the salmon and vegetables. Cover with the lid and cook on low for 1½—2 hours or until the fish is tender and the soup is piping hot.

Lift out the fish with a fish slice and transfer it to a plate. Flake it into chunky pieces, discarding the skin and any bones. Return the fish to the slow cooker pot and add the mangetout. Re-cover and cook on high for 10 minutes or until the mangetout are just tender, then ladle the soup into bowls and garnish with coriander leaves.

For salmon in aromatic Thai broth, follow the recipe as above, adding 3 teaspoons Thai red curry paste, 3 small kaffir lime leaves and 2 teaspoons fish sauce instead of the miso and mirin.

minestrone primavera

Preparation time **20 minutes**
Cooking temperature **high**
Cooking time **5½–7 hours**
Serves **4**

1 **chicken carcass**
1 **onion**, cut into chunks
2 **carrots**, thickly sliced
2 **rosemary sprigs**
2 **bay leaves**
1.5 litres (2½ pints)
  boiling water
250 g (8 oz) **tomatoes**,
  skinned if liked, and diced
1 **red pepper**, cored,
  deseeded and diced
75 g (3 oz) **purple sprouting
  broccoli**, thinly sliced
75 g (3 oz) **runner beans**,
  thinly sliced
75 g (3 oz) small **pasta shells**
handful of **basil**, finely
  chopped
salt and **pepper**
grated **Parmesan cheese**,
  to serve

Preheat the slow cooker if necessary; see the manufacturer's instructions. Break the chicken carcass in half, then add it to the slow cooker pot with the onion, carrots and herbs. Pour over the boiling water and season with salt and pepper.

Cover with the lid and cook on high for 5–6 hours. Strain the stock and return it immediately to the slow cooker pot and re-cover. Strip any meat from the carcass, then add it to the slow cooker pot with the tomatoes, red pepper, broccoli, runner beans and pasta.

Re-cover and cook for 30–60 minutes or until the vegetables are tender. Stir in the basil, taste and adjust the seasoning, if needed. Ladle into bowls and top with a little grated Parmesan. Serve with warm French bread, if liked.

For minestrone verde, make up the soup as above, replacing the red pepper with 1 cored, deseeded and diced green pepper. Add 100 g (3½ oz) finely shredded spinach for the final 10 minutes of cooking.

chicken noodle broth

Preparation time **10 minutes**
Cooking temperature **high**
Cooking time **5 hours 20 minutes–7½ hours**
Serves **4**

1 **chicken carcass**
1 **onion**, cut into wedges
2 **carrots**, sliced
2 **celery sticks**, sliced
1 **bouquet garni**
1.2 litres (2 pints) **boiling water**
75 g (3 oz) **vermicelli pasta**
4 tablespoons chopped **parsley**
salt and **pepper**

Preheat the slow cooker if necessary; see the manufacturer's instructions. Place the chicken carcass in the slow cooker pot, breaking it into 2 pieces if necessary to make it fit. Add the onion, carrots, celery and bouquet garni. Pour over the boiling water and season to taste. Cover and cook on high for 5–7 hours until the vegetables are tender.

Strain the soup through a large sieve, then return the liquid to the slow cooker pot. Remove any meat from the carcass and add it to the pot. Adjust the seasoning if necessary, add the pasta and cook for a further 20–30 minutes until the pasta is just cooked. Sprinkle with the parsley, ladle into deep bowls and serve.

For chicken & minted pea soup, follow the recipe above to make the soup, omitting the pasta, then strain and pour it back into the slow cooker pot. Add 200 g (7 oz) finely sliced leeks, 375 g (12 oz) frozen peas and a small bunch of mint, re-cover and cook for a further 30 minutes. Purée the soup in a blender or with a hand-held stick blender, then stir in 150 g (5 oz) mascarpone cheese until melted. Ladle into bowls and sprinkle with extra mint, if liked.

country mushroom & bacon soup

Preparation time **20 minutes**
Cooking temperature **low**
Cooking time **8 hours**
   5 minutes–9 hours
   10 minutes
Serves **4**

25 g (1 oz) **butter**
1 tablespoon **olive oil**
1 **onion**, chopped
4 **smoked streaky bacon
  rashers**, diced
900 ml (1 ½ pints) **vegetable
  stock**
1 tablespoon **balsamic
  vinegar**
300 g (10 oz) **cup
  mushrooms**, sliced
15 g (½ oz) **dried mixed
  mushrooms**, larger
  pieces sliced
1 **potato**, about 225 g
  (7½ oz), cut into small cubes
40 g (1½ oz) **pearl barley**
2 **thyme sprigs**
150 ml (¼ pint) **double cream**
few extra **thyme leaves** or
  a little chopped **parsley**,
  to garnish
salt and **pepper**

Preheat the slow cooker if necessary; see the manufacturer's instructions. Heat the butter and oil in a saucepan, add the onion and bacon and fry over a medium heat for 5 minutes, stirring, until lightly browned.

Pour in the stock, add the balsamic vinegar, then season well with salt and pepper and bring to the boil, stirring.

Add the fresh and dried mushrooms to the slow cooker pot, then add the potato, barley and thyme. Pour the hot stock mixture into the slow cooker and stir together. Cover and cook on low for 8–9 hours until the bacon and vegetables are tender.

Stir in the cream, taste and adjust the seasoning, if needed. Re-cover and cook for 5–10 minutes until the cream is heated through. Ladle into shallow bowls, discarding the thyme sprigs and adding a few extra thyme leaves or a little chopped parsley. Serve with warm crusty bread, if liked.

For country vegetable & bacon soup, fry the onion and bacon as above. Add the stock and seasoning and omit the vinegar. Add 300 g (10 oz) mixed diced swede, carrot, leek and fresh mushrooms, then the dried mushrooms and remaining ingredients. Cook and serve as above.

chunky chickpea & chorizo soup

Preparation time **20 minutes**
Cooking temperature **low**
Cooking time **6–8 hours**
Serves **4**

2 tablespoons **olive oil**
1 **onion**, chopped
2 **garlic cloves**, finely chopped
150 g (5 oz) **chorizo**, diced
½ teaspoon **hot smoked
    paprika**
2–3 **thyme sprigs**
1 litre (1¾ pints) **chicken
    stock**
1 tablespoon **tomato purée**
375 g (12 oz) **sweet
    potatoes**, peeled and diced
410 g (13½ oz) can
    chickpeas, drained
salt and **pepper**
chopped **parsley** or extra
    thyme leaves, to garnish

Preheat the slow cooker if necessary; see the manufacturer's instructions. Heat the oil in a frying pan, add the onion and fry, stirring, for 5 minutes or until just beginning to turn golden.

Stir in the garlic and chorizo and cook for 2 minutes. Mix in the paprika, add the thyme, stock and tomato purée and bring to the boil, stirring, then season with a little salt and pepper.

Add the sweet potatoes and chickpeas to the slow cooker pot and pour over the hot stock mixture. Cover with the lid and cook on low for 6–8 hours until the sweet potatoes are tender.

Ladle into bowls, sprinkle with a little chopped parsley or extra thyme and serve with warm pitta breads, if liked.

For tomato, chickpea & chorizo soup, make the soup as above up to the point where the paprika and thyme have been added. Reduce the stock to 750 ml (1¼ pints) and add to the frying pan with the tomato purée and 2 teaspoons brown sugar. Bring to the boil. Omit the sweet potatoes but add 500 g (1 lb) skinned and diced tomatoes to the slow cooker pot along with the chickpeas. Pour over the stock mixture and continue as above.

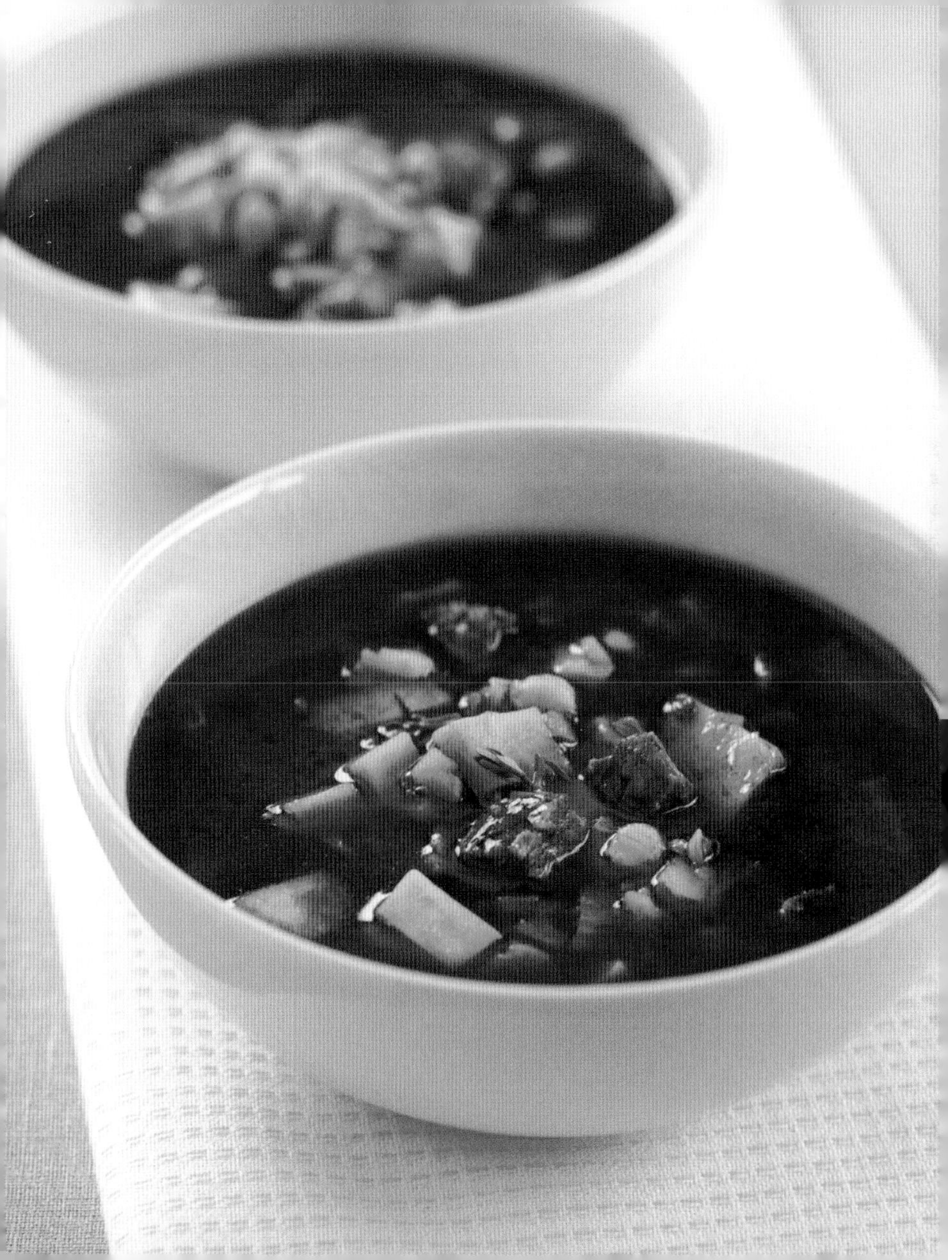

rustic sausage & kale soup

Preparation time **25 minutes**
Cooking temperature **low**
Cooking time **8 hours 20 minutes–9½ hours**
Serves **4**

2 tablespoons **olive oil**
6 **garlicky Toulouse-style sausages**, about 400 g (13 oz) in total, thickly sliced
1 **onion**, chopped
1 **potato**, about 250 g (8 oz), diced
2 **carrots**, diced
400 g (13 oz) can **chopped tomatoes**
1 tablespoon **balsamic vinegar**
450 ml (¾ pint) **chicken** or **pork stock**
2 **rosemary sprigs**
250 g (8 oz) pack **ready-cooked green lentils**, drained if needed
100 g (3½ oz) shredded **green kale**
salt and **pepper**

Preheat the slow cooker if necessary; see the manufacturer's instructions. Heat the oil in a saucepan, add the sausages and fry over a medium heat for 5 minutes until they are just beginning to brown. Stir in the onion, potato and carrot and cook for a further 5 minutes until the vegetables are beginning to soften.

Pour in the tomatoes, vinegar and stock, then add the rosemary and salt and pepper. Bring to the boil, stirring.

Tip the lentils into the base of the slow cooker pot. Pour over the hot tomato mix, then press the sausages and vegetables beneath the liquid. Cover and cook on low for 8–9 hours or until the potatoes are tender and the sausages are cooked through.

Stir in the kale, re-cover the slow cooker and cook for 20–30 minutes until the kale is bright green and just tender. Taste and adjust the seasoning, if needed. Ladle into shallow bowls and serve with hot garlic bread, if liked.

For rustic sausage & pea soup, make up the soup as above, using 6 herb sausages instead of the garlicky Toulouse-style sausages. Add 100 g (3½ oz) frozen peas instead of the kale, re-cover and cook for 20–30 minutes on low.

harira

Preparation time **20 minutes**
Cooking temperature **high**
Cooking time **5–6 hours**
Serves **4**

1 tablespoon **olive oil**
1 **onion**, chopped
2 **garlic cloves**, finely chopped
1 teaspoon **mild paprika**
1 teaspoon **turmeric**
½ teaspoon **ground cumin**
½ teaspoon **ground cinnamon**
600 ml (1 pint) **lamb stock**
1 tablespoon **tomato purée**
350 g (11½ oz) **lamb shank**
1 **potato**, diced
2 **celery sticks**, diced
2 **carrots**, diced
350 g (11½ oz) **tomatoes**, skinned if liked, diced
410 g (13½ oz) can **chickpeas**, drained
salt and **pepper**

To garnish
handful of **mint**, roughly chopped
handful of **parsley**, roughly chopped

Preheat the slow cooker if necessary; see the manufacturer's instructions. Heat the oil in a saucepan, add the onion and fry for 5 minutes, stirring, until softened. Stir in the garlic and spices and cook for 1 minute.

Pour in the stock, add the tomato purée and season with salt and pepper. Bring to the boil, stirring.

Add the lamb shank to the slow cooker pot with the potato, celery, carrots and tomatoes, then tip in the drained chickpeas.

Pour the hot stock mixture into the slow cooker pot. Cover and cook on high for 5–6 hours or until the lamb is beginning to fall off the bone.

Lift the lamb out of the slow cooker pot, take the meat off the bone, cut it into small pieces, discarding any fat, then return it to the slow cooker pot. Sprinkle with the chopped herbs, taste and adjust the seasoning, if needed. Ladle into bowls and serve with warm crusty bread, if liked.

For vegetable harira, omit the lamb shank and lamb stock and replace with 600 ml (1 pint) vegetable stock and 1 red pepper, cored, deseeded and diced. Cook as above, then add 150 g (5 oz) frozen broad or edamame beans for the final 20–30 minutes of cooking.

kids'
favourites

tuna pasta bake

Preparation time **30 minutes**
Cooking temperature **low**
Cooking time **5–6 hours**
Serves **4**

1 tablespoon **olive oil**
1 **onion**, chopped
2 **garlic cloves**, finely chopped
1 **red pepper**, cored,
   deseeded and diced
1 **green pepper**, cored,
   deseeded and diced
2 **celery sticks**, diced
400 g (13 oz) can
   chopped tomatoes
150 ml (¼ pint) **vegetable
   stock**
1 tablespoon **tomato purée**
2 teaspoons **caster sugar**
200 g (7 oz) can **tuna in
   spring water**, drained
handful of **basil leaves**,
   plus extra to garnish
250 g (8 oz) **dried pasta
   twists**
200 g (7 oz) **mozzarella
   cheese**
freshly grated **Parmesan
   cheese**
salt and **pepper**

Preheat the slow cooker if necessary; see the manufacturer's instructions. Heat the oil in a frying pan, add the onion and fry for 5 minutes until softened. Stir in the garlic, diced peppers and celery.

Mix in the canned tomatoes, stock, tomato purée and sugar and season with salt and pepper. Bring to the boil, stirring.

Pour the sauce into the slow cooker pot, add the tuna, broken into chunky pieces, and sprinkle over some of the basil leaves, torn into pieces. Cover with the lid and cook on low for 5–6 hours until the tuna is tender.

When almost ready, add the pasta to a saucepan of boiling water, cook for 8–10 minutes until just tender, then drain. Stir the pasta into the tuna sauce and sprinkle the top with the mozzarella, drained and torn into pieces, a little grated Parmesan and a few of the smallest basil leaves. If liked, you can then lift out the cooking pot using oven gloves and brown the top under a preheated hot grill. Serve sprinkled with extra basil leaves.

For chicken pasta bake, add 500 g (1 lb) raw chicken breast strips, cut into small pieces, in place of the canned tuna and cook on low for 8–9 hours until the chicken is thoroughly cooked through. Serve as above.

chicken, tomato & pesto hotpot

Preparation time **30 minutes**
Cooking temperature **high**
Cooking time **6–7 hours**
Serves **4**

1 tablespoon **olive oil**
625 g (1¼ lb) **boneless,
  skinless chicken thighs**,
  cut into chunks
1 **onion**, chopped
1 tablespoon **plain flour**
2 **garlic cloves**, finely chopped
1 **red pepper**, cored,
  deseeded and diced
1 **yellow pepper**, cored,
  deseeded and diced
100 g (3½ oz) **button
  mushrooms**, sliced
400 g (13 oz) can **chopped
  tomatoes**
300 ml (½ pint) **chicken stock**
2 teaspoons **pesto**
625 g (1¼ lb) **potatoes**,
  thinly sliced
20 g (¾ oz) **butter** (optional)
salt and **pepper**

Preheat the slow cooker if necessary; see the manufacturer's instructions. Heat the oil in a saucepan, add the chicken and onion and fry for 5 minutes, stirring until the chicken is lightly browned.

Stir in the flour, then mix in the garlic, peppers and mushrooms. Add the tomatoes, stock and 1 teaspoon of the pesto, then season with salt and pepper and bring to the boil, stirring.

Transfer to the slow cooker pot. Place the potato slices on top, arranging them so they overlap, then press them lightly into the stock. Spread the potatoes with the remaining pesto and a little extra salt and pepper, then cover with the lid and cook on high for 6–7 hours or until the potatoes are tender when pierced with a knife.

Serve as it is, or dot the top of the potatoes with the butter, then lift the slow cooker pot out of the machine using oven gloves and brown the tops of the potatoes under a preheated hot grill. Serve with steamed green beans, if liked.

For chicken, tomato & bacon hotpot, fry the chicken and onion with 125 g (4 oz) diced streaky bacon. Add the garlic, peppers and mushrooms, then the tomatoes, stock and 1 teaspoon mixed dried herbs instead of the pesto. Add the potato topping and sprinkle with a little extra dried herbs. Cook as above and garnish with fresh chopped parsley.

chicken & chorizo risotto

Preparation time **20 minutes**
Cooking temperature **low**
Cooking time **6–7¼ hours**
Serves **4**

1 tablespoon **olive oil**
500 g (1 lb) **boneless,
    skinless chicken thighs**,
    diced
100 g (3½ oz) **chorizo
    sausage**, diced
2 **garlic cloves**, finely chopped
1 **red pepper**, cored,
    deseeded and sliced
1 **yellow pepper**, cored,
    deseeded and sliced
2 **rosemary sprigs**
1.2 litres (2 pints) **boiling
    chicken stock**
250 g (8 oz) **risotto rice**
150 g (5 oz) **frozen peas**
salt and **pepper**
grated **Cheddar or Parmesan
    cheese**, to serve (optional)

Preheat the slow cooker if necessary; see the manufacturer's instructions. Heat the oil in a frying pan, add the chicken and fry for 4–5 minutes, stirring, until just beginning to brown. Mix in the chorizo and garlic and cook for 2 minutes.

Tip the chicken mixture into the slow cooker pot, then add the peppers and rosemary. Pour in the boiling stock, season with salt and pepper and stir together.

Cover and cook on low for 5–6 hours until the chicken is cooked through. Stir in the risotto rice, cover and cook for 45–60 minutes. Stir in the frozen peas, re-cover and cook for 15 minutes until the peas are hot and the rice is tender. Discard the rosemary. Spoon the risotto into shallow bowls and top with a little grated cheese, if liked.

For turkey & bacon risotto, replace the chicken with 500 g (1 lb) diced, skinless turkey breast meat and the chorizo with 125 g (4 oz) diced smoked back bacon. Add the remaining ingredients and make up the risotto as above.

chicken & mango curry

Preparation time **25 minutes**
Cooking temperature **low**
Cooking time **8–9 hours**
Serves **4**

2 **onions**, quartered
1 **dessert apple**, cored
5 cm (2 inch) piece of
   fresh root ginger, peeled
   and sliced
2 **garlic cloves**, halved
25 g (1 oz) **butter**
3 tablespoons **korma
   curry paste**
3 tablespoons **mango
   chutney**
1 teaspoon **turmeric**
750 g (1½ lb) **boneless,
   skinless chicken thighs**,
   cubed
50 g (2 oz) **red lentils**
500 ml (17 fl oz) **boiling
   chicken stock**
150 ml (¼ pint) **double cream**
salt and **pepper**

Preheat the slow cooker if necessary; see the manufacturer's instructions. Finely chop the onion, apple, ginger and garlic in a food processor, if you have one, or using a large knife.

Heat the butter in a frying pan, add the onion mix and fry gently for 3–4 minutes until softened. Stir in the curry paste, chutney and turmeric, then season with a little salt and pepper.

Add the chicken and lentils to the slow cooker pot, spoon over the onion mix, then pour in the boiling chicken stock and mix together. Press the pieces of chicken beneath the liquid, then cover with the lid and cook on low for 8–9 hours until the chicken is cooked through and the lentils are soft.

Stir the cream into the curry, then spoon into shallow dishes and serve accompanied by steamed basmati rice, if liked, and topped with spoonfuls of mango sambal, if liked (see below).

For mango sambal, to serve as an accompaniment, mix together 1 mango, cut in 3 and stoned, diced and peeled, 2 finely chopped spring onions, 150 g (5 oz) dried coconut shavings, the grated rind and juice of 1 lime, ½–1 halved, deseeded and finely chopped red chilli (to taste) and a small handful of coriander, finely chopped.

spicy turkey tortillas

Preparation time **20 minutes**
Cooking temperature **low**
Cooking time **8–10 hours**
Serves **4**

1 tablespoon **olive oil**
400 g (13 oz) **minced
turkey breast**
1 **onion**, chopped
2 **garlic cloves**, finely chopped
1 teaspoon **dried chilli flakes**
1 teaspoon **cumin seeds**,
crushed
1 teaspoon **mild paprika**
400 g (13 oz) can **chopped
tomatoes**
200 g (7 oz) can **red kidney
beans**, drained
150 ml (¼ pint) **chicken stock**
1 tablespoon **tomato purée**
1 **red pepper**, cored,
deseeded and diced
salt and **pepper**

To serve
4 x 20 cm (8 inch) **soft
tortilla wraps**
50 g (2 oz) **salad leaves**
4 tablespoons **Greek yogurt**
40 g (1½ oz) **Cheddar
cheese**, grated
fresh coriander leaves, torn

Preheat the slow cooker if necessary; see the manufacturer's instructions. Put the oil into a large frying pan and place the pan over a high heat until hot. Add the minced turkey and onion and fry for 4–5 minutes, stirring and breaking up the mince with a wooden spoon, until it is just beginning to brown.

Stir in the garlic, chilli, cumin seeds and paprika, then add the tomatoes, kidney beans, stock and tomato purée. Add the red pepper, season with salt and pepper and bring to the boil. Transfer to the slow cooker pot, cover and cook on low for 8–10 hours until the turkey is cooked through.

Warm the tortillas for 1–2 minutes on each side in a hot, dry frying pan, then place on 4 serving plates. Spoon the spicy turkey on top, then add a handful of salad leaves to each, a spoonful of yogurt, a little Cheddar and top with some torn coriander. Serve immediately.

For spicy turkey thatch, follow the recipe above to make and cook the spicy turkey mixture. Cook, drain and mash 750 g (1½ lb) potatoes, stir in 4 tablespoons vegetable stock and season to taste. Place the turkey mixture in a shallow heatproof dish and spoon the mashed potato on top. Rough up the top with a fork, then brush with ½ beaten egg. Brown under the grill before serving.

monday sausage stew

Preparation time **20 minutes**
Cooking temperature **low**
Cooking time **7–8 hours**
Serves **4**

500 g (1 lb) **pork chipolatas**
1 **onion**, chopped
2 x 415 g (13½ oz) cans
  baked beans
2 tablespoons **Worcestershire
  sauce**
1 teaspoon **dried mixed
  herbs**
1 teaspoon **Dijon mustard**
200 ml (7 fl oz) **boiling
  chicken stock**
300 g (10 oz) **ready-prepared
  pumpkin** or **butternut
  squash,** cut into 2 cm
  (¾ inch) cubes
salt and **pepper**

Preheat the slow cooker if necessary; see the
manufacturer's instructions. Grill the sausages on
one side only.

Meanwhile, add the onion, baked beans and
Worcestershire sauce to the slow cooker pot. Stir
in the herbs, mustard and boiling stock, then mix in
the pumpkin or squash. Season with salt and pepper.

Arrange the sausages on top, with the browned
sides uppermost. Press them into the liquid, then
cover with the lid and cook on low for 7–8 hours until
the sausages are cooked through and the pumpkin or
squash is tender. Spoon into shallow bowls and serve
with garlic bread, if liked.

For chillied sausage stew, grill 500 g (1 lb) chillied
pork sausages or plain chipolatas. Add the onion and
2 x 415 g (13½ oz) cans mixed beans in chilli sauce
to the slow cooker pot, omitting the Worcestershire
sauce, dried herbs and Dijon mustard. Mix in the boiling
stock and pumpkin or squash and cook as above.
Garnish with 3 tablespoons chopped parsley.

sticky ribs

Preparation time **20 minutes**
Cooking temperature **high**
Cooking time **5-6 hours**
Serves **4**

1.4 kg (2¾ lb) **pork ribs**
1 **onion**, quartered
2 **carrots**, thickly sliced
1 teaspoon **dried mixed herbs**
2 tablespoons **malt vinegar**
1 litre (1¾ pints) **boiling water**
salt and **pepper**

Glaze
2 tablespoons **tomato ketchup**
2 tablespoons **thick-set honey**
2 tablespoons **Worcestershire sauce**
1 teaspoon **Dijon mustard**

Preheat the slow cooker if necessary; see the manufacturer's instructions. Add the ribs, onion and carrots to the slow cooker pot, then scatter over the dried herbs. Mix the vinegar into the boiling water, pour the mixture into the pot, then season with salt and pepper.

Cover and cook on high for 5-6 hours or until the meat is almost falling off the bone.

Line the grill pan with foil, lift the ribs out of the slow cooker pot with a draining spoon, arrange them in a single layer on the foil, then add a ladleful of the cooking liquid.

Mix the tomato ketchup, honey, Worcestershire sauce and mustard together, then brush the mixture over the ribs. Cook under a medium grill for 10 minutes, turning and brushing once or twice until covered with a sticky glaze.

Arrange the ribs on serving plates and serve with coleslaw and baked beans, if liked.

For cola ribs, bring 1 litre (1¾ pints) cola to the boil in a saucepan, then pour it over the ribs and vegetables instead of the vinegar and boiling water. Cover, cook and glaze as above.

sausage tagliatelle

Preparation time **25 minutes**
Cooking temperature **low**
Cooking time **8–10 hours**
Serves **4**

1 tablespoon **sunflower oil**
8 **chilli** or **spicy sausages**
1 **onion**, chopped
150 g (5 oz) **cup mushrooms**,
  sliced
2 **garlic cloves**, finely chopped
400 g (13 oz) can **chopped**
  tomatoes
150 ml (¼ pint) **beef stock**
250 g (8 oz) **tagliatelle**
salt and **pepper**
basil leaves, to garnish

Preheat the slow cooker if necessary; see the manufacturer's instructions. Heat the oil in a large frying pan, add the sausages and fry, turning, until browned but not cooked through. Transfer the sausages to the slow cooker pot using tongs.

Drain off the excess fat from the frying pan to leave 2 teaspoons, then add the onion and fry until softened. Mix in the mushrooms and garlic and fry for 1–2 minutes.

Stir in the chopped tomatoes, stock and a little salt and pepper and bring to the boil, stirring. Pour the mixture over the sausages, cover with the lid and cook on low for 8–10 hours until the sausages are cooked through.

Bring a large saucepan of water to the boil. Add the tagliatelle and cook for 7–8 minutes or until just tender, then drain. Lift the sausages out of the slow cooker pot and slice thickly, then return them to the pot with the pasta and mix together. Sprinkle with torn basil leaves and grated Parmesan, if liked.

For chicken & chorizo tagliatelle, omit the sausages and fry 500 g (1 lb) diced boneless chicken thighs in 1 tablespoon olive oil until golden. Drain and transfer to the slow cooker pot. Continue as above, adding 100 g (3½ oz) diced chorizo sausage to the frying pan with the onions and replacing the beef stock with 150 ml (¼ pint) chicken stock.

spanish meatballs

Preparation time **20 minutes**
Cooking temperature **low**
Cooking time **8¼–9¼ hours**
Serves **4**

1 tablespoon **olive oil**
1 **onion,** chopped
75 g (3 oz) **chorizo,** diced
1 teaspoon **mild paprika**
½ teaspoon **ground cumin**
400 g (13 oz) can **chopped tomatoes**
200 ml (7 fl oz) **chicken stock**
2 x 400 g (13 oz) packs of 12 fresh **turkey meatballs**
125 g (4 oz) **frozen peas**
salt and **pepper**

Preheat the slow cooker if necessary; see the manufacturer's instructions. Heat the oil in a saucepan, add the onion and chorizo and fry for 5 minutes until the onions are golden. Stir in the paprika and cumin, then the tomatoes and stock. Season with salt and pepper and bring to the boil, stirring.

Add the meatballs to the slow cooker pot and pour over the hot sauce. Cover and cook on low for 8–9 hours until the meatballs are cooked through.

Stir the meatballs and sprinkle the frozen peas over the top, re-cover and cook for 15 minutes. Gently stir the meatballs again, then serve spooned into rice-lined bowls, if liked.

For spicy beef meatballs, fry the onion with 125 g (4 oz) sliced closed cup mushrooms, omitting the chorizo. Add the spices, tomatoes, 200 ml (7 fl oz) beef stock and seasoning. Add 2 packs of 12 fresh beef meatballs to the slow cooker pot, then pour over the hot sauce. Cook as above, adding the peas, and serve with cooked spaghetti and a little chopped basil.

take 5 spaghetti bolognese

Preparation time **25 minutes**
Cooking temperature **low**
Cooking time **8–9 hours**
Serves **4**

1 tablespoon **olive oil**
500 g (1 lb) **lean minced beef**
1 **onion**, chopped
500 g (1 lb) **passata**
2 **garlic cloves**, finely chopped
1 **courgette**, coarsely grated
1 **carrot**, coarsely grated
1 **red pepper**, cored,
  deseeded and diced
150 g (5 oz) **cup mushrooms**,
  chopped
200 ml (7 fl oz) **beef stock**
1 teaspoon **dried oregano**
250 g (8 oz) **dried spaghetti**
salt and **pepper**
small handful of **basil leaves**,
  to garnish

Preheat the slow cooker if necessary; see the manufacturer's instructions. Heat the oil in a saucepan, add the mince and onion and fry for 5 minutes, stirring, until the mince is evenly browned.

Stir in the passata, garlic and the grated and chopped vegetables, then mix in the stock and oregano and season with salt and pepper. Bring to the boil, stirring.

Pour the mixture into the slow cooker pot. Press the meat and vegetables into the liquid to submerge them, then cover with the lid and cook on low for 8–9 hours until the beef and vegetables are tender.

Once the bolognese sauce is ready, bring a saucepan of water to the boil, add the spaghetti and cook for 8–10 minutes or until tender. Drain, then stir the pasta into the Bolognese sauce. Spoon into shallow bowls and garnish with basil leaves and grated Parmesan, if liked.

For turkey Bolognese, omit the beef and fry 500 g (1 lb) minced turkey leg or breast meat with the onion. Add the remaining ingredients, using 300 ml (½ pint) chicken stock instead of the beef stock. Cook and serve as above.

cheese-topped cottage pie

Preparation time **35 minutes**
Cooking temperature **low**
Cooking time **8–9 hours**
Serves **4**

1 tablespoon **sunflower oil**
500 g (1 lb) **lean minced beef**
1 **onion**, chopped
375 g (12 oz) diced **carrot**
and **swede**
415 g (13½ oz) can **baked
beans**
300 ml (½ pint) **beef stock**
1 tablespoon **Worcestershire
sauce**
1 teaspoon **dried mixed
herbs**
1 kg (2 lb) **potatoes**, cut
into chunks
50 g (2 oz) **butter**
1 **egg**, beaten
3–4 tablespoons **milk**
125 g (4 oz) **Cheddar
cheese**, grated
salt and **pepper**

Preheat the slow cooker if necessary; see the manufacturer's instructions. Heat the oil in a saucepan, add the mince and onion and fry for 5 minutes, stirring, until the mince is evenly browned.

Stir in the diced vegetables, baked beans, stock and Worcestershire sauce, then mix in the herbs and season with salt and pepper. Bring to the boil, stirring.

Spoon the mixture into the slow cooker pot, cover with the lid and cook on low for 8–9 hours until the beef and vegetables are tender.

When you are almost ready to serve, add the potatoes to a saucepan of boiling water, cook for 15 minutes or until tender, then drain and return to the pan. Mash well, then mix in the butter, beaten egg and enough of the milk to make a smooth mash. Stir in two-thirds of the cheese and season with salt and pepper.

Transfer the mince mixture from the slow cooker to 4 individual ovenproof dishes, spoon the cheesy mash on top, rough up with a fork and sprinkle with the remaining cheese. Cook under a preheated hot grill until the cheese is bubbling and golden. Serve with peas, if liked.

For cheesy-topped turkey pie, omit the beef and fry 500 g (1 lb) minced turkey leg or breast meat with the onion as above. Stir in the diced vegetables, baked beans, 300 ml (½ pint) chicken stock and the Worcestershire sauce, then mix in the herbs and season. Continue as above.

jumbo burger with tomato sauce

Preparation time **25 minutes**
Cooking temperature **high**
Cooking time **3–4 hours**
Serves **4**

oil, for greasing
1 bunch of **spring onions**, chopped
250 g (8 oz) **lean minced beef**
250 g (8 oz) **lean herby sausages**, skins removed
4 tablespoons **fresh breadcrumbs**
2 tablespoons **Worcestershire sauce**
400 g (13 oz) can **chopped tomatoes**
125 ml (4 fl oz) **vegetable stock**
1 teaspoon **English mustard**
1 tablespoon **light muscovado sugar**
1 **green** or **red pepper**, cored, deseeded and diced
salt and **pepper**

To serve
4 **burger buns**, halved
shredded lettuce

Preheat the slow cooker if necessary; see the manufacturer's instructions. Grease the inside of 2 x 350 ml (12 fl oz) soufflé dishes with a diameter of 10 cm (4 inches) and a height of 6 cm (2½ inches) with a little oil. Line the bases with nonstick baking paper.

Add half the spring onions, the beef, sausagemeat and breadcrumbs to a bowl or food processor. Add 1 tablespoon of the Worcestershire sauce, season with salt and pepper and mix together. Divide between the 2 dishes and press down well to level off the surface. Cover with foil and put the dishes side by side in the slow cooker pot.

Add the tomatoes, stock, remaining Worcestershire sauce, mustard and sugar to a small saucepan. Season with salt and pepper and bring to the boil. Stir in the remaining spring onions and the green or red pepper and spoon the mixture into the gaps around the dishes.

Cover with the lid and cook on high for 3–4 hours until the burgers are cooked. Test with a skewer to make sure the juices do not run pink. Lift the burger dishes out of the slow cooker with oven gloves, pour the excess fat from the dishes, then turn the burgers out.

Split the burger buns and add lettuce to the bottom halves. Cut the burgers in half horizontally. Place 1 half on each bun, then top with spoonfuls of the tomato sauce and serve the remaining sauce in a small bowl. Accompany with microwave or oven chips, if liked.

For turkey burger & tomato sauce, omit the minced beef and add 250 g (8 oz) minced turkey leg meat. Make and cook as above.

chillied beef with cheesy tortillas

Preparation time **20 minutes**
Cooking temperature **low**
Cooking time **8–10 hours**
Serves **4**

1 tablespoon **sunflower oil**
500 g (1 lb) **extra-lean minced beef**
1 **onion**, chopped
2 **garlic cloves**, finely chopped
1 teaspoon **smoked paprika**
½ teaspoon **crushed dried red chillies**
1 teaspoon **ground cumin**
1 tablespoon **plain flour**
400 g (13 oz) can **chopped tomatoes**
410 g (13½ oz) can **red kidney beans**, drained
150 ml (¼ pint) **beef stock**
1 tablespoon **dark muscovado sugar**
salt and **pepper**

Topping
100 g (3½ oz) **tortilla chips**
½ **red pepper**, cored, deseeded and diced
chopped **coriander**
100 g (3½ oz) **mature Cheddar cheese**, grated

Preheat the slow cooker if necessary; see the manufacturer's instructions. Heat the oil in a frying pan, add the mince and onion and fry, stirring, for 5 minutes, breaking up the mince with a spoon, until it is browned.

Stir in the garlic, paprika, chillies and cumin and cook for 2 minutes. Stir in the flour. Mix in the tomatoes, kidney beans, stock and sugar, season with salt and pepper and pour the mixture into the slow cooker pot. Cover with the lid and cook on low for 8–10 hours until the beef is tender.

Stir the chilli, then arrange the tortilla chips on top. Sprinkle over the remaining topping ingredients, lift the pot out of the housing using oven gloves and brown the chilli under a preheated hot grill until the cheese just melts. Spoon into bowls to serve.

For turkey fajitas with guacamole, make up the chilli as above using 500 g (1 lb) minced turkey instead of the beef. To serve, halve, stone and peel 1 avocado and mash the flesh with the juice of 1 lime, a small bunch of torn fresh coriander and some salt and pepper. Spoon the turkey mixture on to 8 warmed, medium soft flour tortillas, top with spoonfuls of the guacamole and 8 tablespoons soured cream and roll up to serve.

spiced lamb wraps

Preparation time **20 minutes**
Cooking temperature **low**
Cooking time **8–9 hours**
Serves **4**

1 tablespoon **olive oil**
500 g (1 lb) **minced lamb**
1 **red onion**, finely chopped
2 teaspoons **ground cumin**
1 teaspoon **ground cinnamon**
½ teaspoon **chilli powder**
1 teaspoon **dried oregano**
1 tablespoon **tomato purée**
75 g (3 oz) **bulgar wheat**
600 ml (1 pint) **boiling
  beef stock**
salt and **pepper**

To serve
8 large **soft flour wraps**
400 g (13 oz) **hummus**
1 **cos lettuce**, shredded
small handful of **mint**,
  finely chopped
½ **cucumber**, cut into strips

Preheat the slow cooker if necessary; see the manufacturer's instructions. Heat the oil in a frying pan, add the mince and onion and fry for 5 minutes, stirring until the mince is evenly browned.

Stir in the ground spices, dried herbs and tomato purée, then season with a little salt and pepper.

Spoon the mixture into the slow cooker pot, add the bulgar wheat, then stir in the boiling stock. Cover with the lid and cook on low for 8–9 hours until the lamb is tender.

When ready to serve, warm the wraps in a dry frying pan or in the microwave according to the packet instructions, then spread each one with a little hummus.

Stir the mince mixture. Spoon it over the wraps, then top with the lettuce, mint and cucumber. Fold in the top and bottom of each wrap, then roll it up tightly to enclose the filling. Cut in half and serve immediately.

For chillied beef wraps, omit the lamb and fry 500 g (1 lb) minced beef with the onion as above. Stir in the spices, herbs and tomato pureé as above, adding ¼–½ teaspoon crushed dried red chillies, to taste. Cook and serve as above.

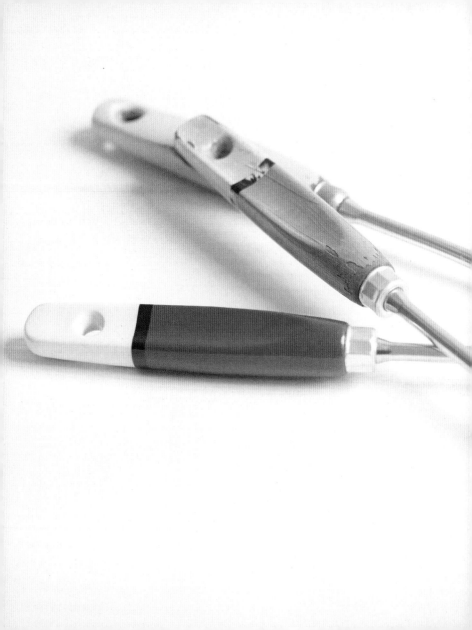

everyday
favourites

balsamic-baked shallots

Preparation time **20 minutes**
Cooking temperature **high**
Cooking time **4–5 hours**
Serves **4**

750 g (1 ½ lb) **shallots**
50 g (2 oz) **butter**, at room
   temperature
2 tablespoons **dark**
   muscovado sugar
2 tablespoons **balsamic**
   vinegar
2 tablespoons **cream sherry**
   (optional)
leaves from 2 **rosemary**
   sprigs
salt and **pepper**

Preheat the slow cooker if necessary; see the manufacturer's instructions. Add the shallots to a large bowl, cover with boiling water and leave to soak for 2–3 minutes to soften the skins.

Lift the shallots out of the water with a draining spoon, peel away the skins and cut any large ones in half.

Spread the butter over the base of the slow cooker pot, add the shallots, then sprinkle over the sugar and drizzle over the vinegar and sherry, if using. Scatter the rosemary leaves on top, season with salt and pepper, then cover with the lid.

Cook on high for 4–5 hours until tender, stirring the shallots once during cooking and again at the end. Serve with grilled sausages and mashed potatoes, if liked.

For shallot tarte tatin, transfer the shallots and cooking juices to a 20 cm (8 inch) frying pan with an ovenproof handle or a cake tin without a loose base. Roll out 250 g (8 oz) puff pastry and trim to a circle a little larger than the pan. Place on top of shallots, tucking the pastry down the sides. Prick the top 2 or 3 times, then place in a preheated oven, 200°C (400°F), Gas Mark 6, for 30 minutes. Cover the pan with a plate, turn out and cut into wedges to serve.

white bean & chipotle chilli

Preparation time **20 minutes**
Cooking temperature **high**
Cooking time **4–5 hours**
Serves **4**

1 **dried chipotle chilli**
3 tablespoons **boiling water**
2 tablespoons **olive oil**
1 **red onion**, roughly chopped
2 **garlic cloves**, finely chopped
½ teaspoon **ground cinnamon**
1 teaspoon **ground cumin**
1 teaspoon **dried oregano**
400 g (13 oz) can **chopped tomatoes**
200 ml (7 fl oz) **vegetable stock**
1 tablespoon **light muscovado sugar**
1 **sweet potato**, peeled and cut into 2 cm (¾ inch) cubes
1 **carrot**, diced
1 **red pepper**, cored, deseeded and diced
200 g (7 oz) **cherry tomatoes**
380 g (12¼ oz) can **cannellini beans**, drained
salt and **pepper**

Add the chilli to a cup or small bowl and soak in the boiling water for 15 minutes. Preheat the slow cooker if necessary; see the manufacturer's instructions. Heat the oil in a frying pan, add the onion and fry for 5 minutes, stirring, until softened and just beginning to brown.

Stir in the garlic, spices and herbs, then add the tomatoes, stock and the sugar. Tip the chilli soaking water into the pan, then finely chop the chilli and stir it in with salt and pepper. Bring to the boil, stirring.

Add the sweet potato, carrot, red pepper and cherry tomatoes to the slow cooker pot, then mix in the cannellini beans. Pour over the hot stock mixture and press the vegetables beneath the liquid as much as you can. Cover with the lid and cook on high for 4–5 hours until the vegetables are tender.

Stir again, then spoon the chilli into bowls and garnish with tortillas and coriander leaves, if liked.

For beef & bean chipotle chilli, fry the onion with 500g (1lb) minced beef. Make up as above, omitting the white cannellini beans and sweet potato and adding a 415g (13½ oz) can of drained red kidney beans instead. Cook on high for 4–5 hours.

quorn jalfrezi

Preparation time **20 minutes**
Cooking temperature **low**
Cooking time **4–5 hours**
Serves **4**

1 **onion**, quartered
2 **garlic cloves**, halved
1 **green finger chilli**, halved
   and deseeded
4 cm (1½ inch) piece of
   fresh root ginger, peeled
   and sliced
handful of **coriander**, plus
   extra to garnish (optional)
4 tablespoons **desiccated
   coconut**
2 tablespoons **sunflower oil**
1 teaspoon **ground coriander**
1 teaspoon **turmeric**
2 teaspoons **garam masala**
1 teaspoon **brown mustard
   seeds**
300 ml (½ pint) **vegetable
   stock**
350 g (11½ oz) **Quorn pieces**
200 g (7 oz) **cherry tomatoes**,
   halved
salt and **pepper**

To serve
rice
naan breads

Preheat the slow cooker if necessary; see the manufacturer's instructions. Finely chop the onion, garlic, chilli, ginger, coriander and coconut together in a food processor if you have one, or using a large knife.

Heat the oil in a frying pan, add the onion mixture and cook over a low heat for 2–3 minutes, stirring, until softened. Stir in the ground spices and mustard seeds, cook for 1 minute, then mix in the stock, season with salt and pepper and bring to the boil.

Add the Quorn pieces and tomatoes to the slow cooker pot, then pour over the hot spice mixture. Cover with the lid and cook on low for 4–5 hours until tender. Serve with rice and naan breads, garnished with the extra coriander and coconut shavings, if liked.

For chicken jalfrezi, omit the Quorn pieces and add 500 g (1 lb) boneless, skinless diced chicken thighs and the tomatoes to the slow cooker pot, pour over the hot spice mixture and cook as above for 8–9 hours until the chicken is cooked through.

salmon & rocket tagliatelle

Preparation time **20 minutes**
Cooking temperature **low**
Cooking time **1¾–2¼ hours**
Serves **4**

4 **salmon fillets**, about
   550 g (1 lb 2 oz) in total
1 **lemon**, sliced
2 small **bay leaves**, torn in half
300 ml (½ pint) **boiling
   fish stock**
500 g (1 lb) **fresh tagliatelle**
250 g (8 oz) **soft cheese with
   garlic and herbs**
120 g (4 oz) bag **mixed
   rocket, watercress and
   spinach leaves**
handful of **basil**, torn into
   pieces
salt and **black pepper**

Preheat the slow cooker if necessary; see the manufacturer's instructions. Arrange the salmon fillets so that they fit snugly in the base of the slow cooker pot. Squeeze the juice from the lemon slices over the salmon, arrange the slices on top with the bay leaves and season with a little salt and pepper.

Pour over the boiling stock, then cover and cook on low for 1¾–2¼ hours until the fish is cooked and flakes easily into even-coloured flakes when pressed with a knife.

When the salmon is ready, put the pasta into a large saucepan of boiling water. Cook for 3 minutes until just tender. Drain into a colander. Ladle 200 ml (7 fl oz) of the hot fish stock from the slow cooker pot into the empty pasta pan, stir in the soft cheese and heat until melted. Add the rocket and other leaves, heat for 2 minutes until just wilted, then stir in the pasta.

Take the pan off the heat and lift the salmon out of the slow cooker. Remove the salmon skin, break the fish into large flakes, discarding any bones, and toss gently with the pasta and torn basil leaves.

Spoon into bowls and top with extra pepper and a little grated Parmesan, if liked.

For smoked cod & rocket tagliatelle, add 550 g (1 lb 2 oz) smoked cod loins to the base of the slow cooker pot, add the bay leaves and boiling fish stock, omitting the lemon. Cook as above. Cook 125 g (4 oz) frozen sweetcorn with the pasta, then drain and continue as above, omitting the basil.

herb-crusted salmon with tomatoes

Preparation time **20 minutes**
Cooking temperature **high**
  and **low**
Cooking time **1¼–1¾ hours**
Serves **4**

500 g (1 lb) **mixed red** and
  yellow cherry tomatoes
  (or all red if preferred),
  halved
200 g (7 oz) canned **chopped
  tomatoes**
1 teaspoon **caster sugar**
handful of **basil**, chopped
4 **salmon fillets**, about 150 g
  (5 oz) each
salt and **pepper**

Topping
2 tablespoons **olive oil**
4 tablespoons **fresh
  breadcrumbs**
4 tablespoons freshly grated
  Parmesan cheese

Preheat the slow cooker if necessary; see the manufacturer's instructions. Add the fresh and canned tomatoes to the base of the slow cooker pot, sprinkle with the sugar and season with salt and pepper, then sprinkle with a little of the chopped basil.

Arrange the salmon in a single layer on top, sprinkle with more chopped basil (reserving 2 tablespoons for the topping) and salt and pepper. Cover with the lid and cook on high for 1¼ hours or until the salmon is opaque and the fish breaks into even-coloured flakes when pressed with a knife. If you are not ready to eat, reduce to low for a further 30 minutes.

When ready to eat, heat the oil in a small frying pan, add the breadcrumbs and Parmesan and fry, stirring, over a medium heat until golden brown and crispy. Stir in the reserved chopped basil.

Spoon the tomatoes into shallow serving dishes, top with the fish and then spoon the crumb topping over. Serve with salad, if liked.

For prosciutto-wrapped cod with cherry tomatoes,
add the tomatoes, sugar, seasoning and basil to the slow cooker pot. Wrap 4 x 150 g (5 oz) pieces of thick cod loin each with 1 slice of prosciutto or Parma ham. Add to the slow cooker in a single layer, sprinkle with basil, then cook and serve as above.

smoked mackerel kedgeree

Preparation time **15 minutes**
Cooking temperature **low**
Cooking time **3¼–4¼ hours**
Serves **4**

1 tablespoon **sunflower oil**
1 **onion**, chopped
1 teaspoon **turmeric**
2 tablespoons **mango
  chutney**
750–900 ml (1¼–1½ pints)
  vegetable stock
1 **bay leaf**
175 g (6 oz) **easy-cook
  brown rice**
3 **smoked mackerel fillets**,
  about 250 g (8 oz) in total,
  skinned
100 g (3½ oz) **frozen peas**
25 g (1 oz) **watercress** or
  rocket leaves
4 **hard-boiled eggs**, cut into
  wedges
salt and **pepper**

Preheat the slow cooker if necessary; see the
manufacturer's instructions. Heat the oil in a frying
pan, add the onion and fry, stirring, for 5 minutes or
until softened and just beginning to turn golden.

Stir in the turmeric, chutney, stock, bay leaf and a little
salt and pepper and bring to the boil. Pour the mixture
into the slow cooker pot and add the rice. Add the
smoked mackerel to the pot in a single layer. Cover
with the lid and cook on low for 3–4 hours or until the
rice is tender and has absorbed almost all the stock.

Mix in the peas. Break up the fish into chunky pieces.
Add extra hot stock if needed to loosen the rice
(it will have absorbed a lot of the cooking liquid by now),
then re-cover and cook for 15 minutes more. Stir in the
watercress or rocket, spoon on to plates and garnish
with wedges of hard-boiled egg.

For smoked haddock kedgeree with cardamom,
make up the recipe as above but omit the mango
chutney and, instead, add 4 crushed cardamom pods
with their black seeds. Replace the smoked mackerel
with 400 g (13 oz) skinned smoked haddock fillet,
cut into 2 pieces. Continue as above, adding the peas
and egg wedges at the end but omitting the rocket or
watercress. Drizzle with 4 tablespoons double cream.

all-in-one chicken casserole

Preparation time **20 minutes**
Cooking temperature **low**
Cooking time **8¼–10¼ hours**
Serves **4**

1 tablespoon **olive oil**
4 **chicken legs**, 875 g (1¾ lb)
  in total
50 g (2 oz) **smoked back
  bacon**, trimmed of fat and
  chopped
300 g (10 oz) **baby new
  potatoes**, thickly sliced
2 **small leeks**, thickly sliced,
  white and green parts
  kept separate
2 **celery sticks**, thickly sliced
2 **carrots**, sliced
2 teaspoons **plain flour**
1 teaspoon **dried mixed
  herbs**
1 teaspoon **mustard powder**
450 ml (¾ pint) **chicken stock**
50 g (2 oz) **curly kale**, sliced
salt and **pepper**

Put half the olive oil into a large frying pan and set it over a high heat. When the pan is hot, add the chicken and cook for 5 minutes, turning, until browned all over. Transfer to the slow cooker pot.

Add the bacon and potatoes to the frying pan with the remaining olive oil and cook for 4–5 minutes, stirring, until the bacon is beginning to brown. Stir in the white leek slices (reserving the green slices), the celery and carrots. Add the flour, herbs and mustard and stir well.

Pour in the stock, season to taste and bring to the boil, stirring. Spoon the mixture over the chicken, cover and cook on low for 8–10 hours or until the chicken is thoroughly cooked and the meat juices run clear when the thickest parts of the leg are pierced with a sharp knife.

Add the reserved green leek slices and the kale to the slow cooker pot, re-cover and cook for 15 minutes until the vegetables are just tender. Serve in shallow bowls.

For chicken hotpot, follow the main recipe to make the chicken mixture, omitting the new potatoes and carrots. Transfer to the slow cooker pot and cover with 300 g (10 oz) scrubbed and thinly sliced baking potatoes and 2 thinly sliced carrots, arranging the slices so that each piece overlaps the next. Dot with 20 g (¾ oz) butter and season to taste, then cook as above. After cooking, brown the top under the grill, if liked.

piri piri chicken

Preparation time **20 minutes**,
  plus overnight marinating
Cooking temperature **low**
Cooking time **8–9 hours**
Serves **4**

625 g (1¼ lb) **boneless,
  skinless chicken thighs,**
  cut into large chunks
2 tablespoons **olive oil**
2 tablespoons **red wine
  vinegar**
1 tablespoon **tomato purée**
1 tablespoon **light
  muscovado sugar**
2 teaspoons **piri piri
  spice blend**
1 **red onion**, finely chopped
2 **garlic cloves**, finely chopped
1 **red pepper**, cored,
  deseeded and diced
1 **yellow pepper**, cored,
  deseeded and diced
400 g (13 oz) can **chopped
  tomatoes**
150 ml (¼ pint) **chicken stock**
1 tablespoon **cornflour**
salt and **pepper**
chopped **parsley**, to garnish

Put the chicken into a large plastic food bag. Mix the
oil, vinegar, tomato purée, sugar and piri piri together
in a bowl with a little salt and pepper. Pour the mixture
into the bag containing the chicken, then add the
onion, garlic and peppers. Seal the bag, then shake the
contents together to mix. Leave to marinate overnight
in the refrigerator.

Preheat the slow cooker if necessary; see the
manufacturer's instructions. Tip the tomatoes and stock
into a small saucepan. Mix the cornflour to a paste with
a little cold water, add the paste to the pan and bring
the mixture to the boil, stirring.

Tip the contents of the food bag into the slow cooker
pot, pour over the hot tomato mixture, then cover and
cook on low for 8–9 hours until the chicken is cooked
through. Stir well, then sprinkle with the parsley and
serve with rice, if liked.

For piri piri vegetables, omit the chicken and chicken
stock. Add 375 g (12 oz) halved, cap mushrooms and
a 415 g (13½ oz) drained can cannellini beans to the
marinade in the bag. Seal and chill overnight, or cook
straight away if it suits you better. Continue and cook
as above.

sweet & sour chicken

Preparation time **20 minutes**
Cooking temperature **low**
Cooking time **7¼–8½ hours**
Serves **4**

1 tablespoon **sunflower oil**

1 kg (2 lb) **boneless, skinless chicken thighs**, cubed

4 **spring onions**, thickly sliced, white and green parts kept separate

2 **carrots**, halved lengthways and thinly sliced

2.5 cm (1 inch) piece of **fresh root ginger**, finely chopped

425 g (14 oz) can **pineapple chunks in natural juice**

300 ml (½ pint) **chicken stock**

1 tablespoon **cornflour**

1 tablespoon **tomato purée**

2 tablespoons **caster sugar**

2 tablespoons **soy sauce**

2 tablespoons **malt vinegar**

225 g (7½ oz) can **bamboo shoots**, drained

125 g (4 oz) **bean sprouts**

100 g (3½ oz) **mangetout**, thinly sliced

Preheat the slow cooker if necessary; see the manufacturer's instructions. Heat the oil in a large frying pan over a high heat, add the chicken and cook for 3–4 minutes until browned on all sides. Add the white spring onion slices (reserving the green slices), the carrots and ginger and cook for 2 minutes.

Stir in the pineapple chunks with their juice and the stock. Put the cornflour, tomato purée and sugar in a small bowl, then mix in the soy sauce and vinegar to make a smooth paste. Add to the pan and bring to the boil, stirring.

Transfer the mixture to the slow cooker pot, add the bamboo shoots and press the chicken pieces into the liquid. Cover and cook on low for 7–8 hours until the chicken is cooked through.

Add the reserved green spring onion slices, the bean sprouts and mangetout and mix well. Re-cover and cook for 15 minutes or until the vegetables are just tender. Serve with boiled rice, if liked.

For chillied sweet & sour chicken, make up the recipe as above, adding 1 deseeded and chopped mild red chilli along with the pineapple. Serve with a little bowl of extra chopped chili to sprinkle over when serving, if liked.

paprika pork & cornmeal dumplings

Preparation time **25 minutes**
Cooking temperature **low**
  and **high**
Cooking time **9–10 hours**
Serves **4**

3 tablespoons **olive oil**
750 g (1½ lb) **boneless pork
  shoulder steaks**, cubed
2 **red onions**, cubed
½–1 teaspoon **hot smoked
  paprika** (to taste)
½ teaspoon **ground cumin**
½ teaspoon **ground cinnamon**
415 g (13½ oz) can **baked
  beans**
400 g (13 oz) can **chopped
  tomatoes**
200 ml (7 fl oz) **beef stock**
300 g (10 oz) **chantenay
  carrots**, larger ones halved
salt and **pepper**

Dumplings
75 g (3 oz) **fine cornmeal**
75 g (3 oz) **plain flour**
1 teaspoon **baking powder**
2 **spring onions**, chopped
100 g (3½ oz) **Cheddar
  cheese**, grated
2 **eggs**
150 g (5 oz) **natural yogurt**

96

Preheat the slow cooker if necessary; see the manufacturer's instructions. Heat 1 tablespoon of the olive oil in a saucepan, then add the pork a few pieces at a time until all the pieces are in the pan. Fry for 5 minutes until the meat is just beginning to brown, then mix in the onions and cook for a few minutes until they just begin to soften.

Stir in the paprika, cumin and cinnamon, then mix in the baked beans, tomatoes and stock. Season with salt and pepper, then bring to the boil, stirring.

Spoon into the slow cooker pot, add the carrots and press the carrots and pork beneath the liquid. Cover with the lid and cook on low for 8–9 hours until the meat and carrots are tender.

Make the dumplings. Put the cornmeal, flour and baking powder in a bowl. Stir in the spring onions, cheese and a little salt and pepper. Add the eggs, yogurt and remaining olive oil and whisk together briefly.

Take the lid off the stew, drop spoonfuls of the dumpling mix over the top, leaving a little space between the spoonfuls if you can. Re-cover with the lid and cook on high for 1 hour until the dumplings are well risen and firm. Take the slow cooker pot out of the machine with oven gloves and brown the top under a preheated grill, if liked. Spoon into shallow bowls and serve with broccoli, if liked.

For paprika beef & wholegrain mustard cornmeal dumplings, fry 750 g (1½ lb) cubed stewing beef in place of the pork, then continue as above. When making the dumplings, add 2 teaspoons wholegrain mustard with the eggs, yogurt and oil. Serve as above.

leek & gammon braise

Preparation time **20 minutes**
Cooking temperature **high**
Cooking time **5¼–6¼ hours**
Serves **4**

750 g (1½ lb) **smoked gammon joint,** well rinsed with cold water
2 **leeks**, thickly sliced, white and green parts kept separate
300 g (10 oz) **baby new potatoes**, scrubbed and larger ones halved
300 g (10 oz) **chantenay carrots**, larger ones halved
1 litre (1¾ pints) **dry cider** or **chicken stock**
1 teaspoon **Dijon mustard**
1 **chicken stock cube**, crumbled (omit this if using chicken stock in place of the dry cider)
2 **bay leaves**
4 **cloves**
1½ tablespoons **cornflour**
pepper
handful of **parsley**, chopped, to garnish

Preheat the slow cooker if necessary, see manufacturer's instructions. Put the gammon joint in the centre of the slow cooker pot, then arrange the white sliced leeks (reserving the green ones), potatoes and carrots around it.

Add the cider or stock, mustard, stock cube, bay leaves and cloves to a saucepan. Season with pepper (don't add salt as the joint may be salty, so better to taste and add at the end) and bring to the boil.

Pour the cider mix into the slow cooker pot, cover with the lid and cook on high for 5–6 hours or until the gammon joint is very tender.

Mix the cornflour to a paste with a little water. Stir the paste into the cider sauce, then add the reserved green leek slices. Re-cover and cook for 15 minutes until the green leek slices are tender and the sauce has thickened slightly.

Lift the gammon joint out of the slow cooker and cut it into thick, rough shreds. Ladle the vegetables and sauce into shallow bowls, add the gammon and sprinkle with the parsley.

For leek & gammon with parsley sauce, omit the cider or chicken stock and cornflour and add 1 litre (1¾ pints) vegetable stock. When the gammon is cooked, pour off 300 ml (½ pint) of the hot stock. Melt 50 g (2 oz) butter in a saucepan, stir in 50 g (2 oz) plain flour, then mix in the measured hot stock and heat, stirring. Mix in 300 ml (½ pint) milk and a large handful of parsley, finely chopped. Cook until thickened. Season. Arrange the gammon and vegetables on serving plates and serve with the sauce.

balsamic pork with red onions

Preparation time **20 minutes**
Cooking temperature **low**
Cooking time **8–9 hours**
Serves **4**

2 tablespoons **olive oil**
6 **boneless pork shoulder
  steaks**, about 800 g (1¾ lb)
  in total, cut into chunks
1 **red onion**, cut into wedges
2 tablespoons **plain flour**
450 ml (¾ pint) **pork** or
  chicken stock
2 tablespoons **balsamic
  vinegar**
1 tablespoon **light
  muscovado sugar**
1 teaspoon **English mustard**
300 g (10 oz) **parsnips**, cut
  into chunks
1 **dessert apple**, cored and
  diced (no need to peel)
salt and **pepper**
chopped **parsley**, to garnish

Preheat the slow cooker if necessary; see the manufacturer's instructions. Heat the oil in a large frying pan, add the pork and fry, stirring, until the meat is evenly browned. Scoop the chunks of pork out of the pan with a draining spoon and add them to the slow cooker pot. Add the onion to the frying pan and fry for 5 minutes until softened.

Stir in the flour, then mix in the stock, then the vinegar, sugar and mustard. Season with salt and pepper. Bring to the boil, stirring. Add the parsnips and apple to the slow cooker pot, pour over the onion and stock mix and press the parsnips beneath the liquid, if needed. Cover and cook on low for 8–9 hours until the pork and parsnips are tender.

Sprinkle with chopped parsley and serve spooned into shallow bowls.

For cider-braised pork with red onions & parsnips,
make up the recipe as above, omitting the balsamic vinegar and using 200 ml (7 fl oz) dry cider and 250 ml (8 fl oz) pork or chicken stock for the cooking liquid.

beef adobo

Preparation time **25 minutes**
Cooking temperature **low**
Cooking time **8–10 hours**
Serves **4**

1 tablespoon **sunflower oil**
750 g (1½ lb) **braising beef**,
    fat discarded and cubed
1 large **onion**, sliced
2 **garlic cloves**, finely
    chopped
2 tablespoons **plain flour**
450 ml (¾ pint) **beef stock**
4 tablespoons **soy sauce**
4 tablespoons **white wine
    vinegar**
1 tablespoon **caster sugar**
2 **bay leaves**
juice of 1 **lime**
salt and **pepper**
rice, to serve

To garnish
1 **carrot**, cut into thin sticks
½ bunch of **spring onions**,
    cut into shreds
coriander leaves

Preheat the slow cooker if necessary; see the manufacturer's instructions. Heat the oil in a large frying pan and add the beef a few pieces at a time until all the meat has been added. Fry over a high heat, turning, until evenly browned, then lift out of the pan with a slotted spoon and transfer the beef to a plate.

Put the onion into the frying pan and fry for 5 minutes or until it is just beginning to brown. Mix in the garlic and cook for 2 minutes. Stir in the flour, then gradually mix in the stock. Add the soy sauce, vinegar, sugar, bay leaves and salt and pepper and bring to the boil, stirring.

Transfer the beef to the slow cooker pot, pour over the onion and stock mixture, cover with the lid and cook on low for 8–10 hours until the beef is tender.

Stir in lime juice to taste. Serve in shallow bowls lined with rice. Garnish with carrot sticks, shredded spring onions and coriander leaves.

For hoisin beef, combine 3 tablespoons each of soy sauce and rice or wine vinegar with 2 tablespoons hoisin sauce and 2.5 cm (1 inch) piece of peeled and finely chopped fresh root ginger. Add this mixture to the beef stock with the sugar. Omit the bay leaves. Bring the mixture to the boil, then continue as above, adding the lime juice just before serving.

beef lasagne

Preparation time **25 minutes**
Cooking temperature **low**
Cooking time **5–6¼ hours**
Serves 4

1 tablespoon **olive oil**
500 g (1 lb) **minced beef**
1 **onion**, chopped
1 **red pepper**, cored,
  deseeded, diced
1 **green pepper**, cored,
  deseeded and diced
125 g (4 oz) **button
  mushrooms**, sliced
2 **celery sticks**, chopped
2 **garlic cloves**, finely chopped
500 g (1 lb) **passata**
200 ml (7 fl oz) **beef stock**
150 ml (¼ pint) **red wine** or
  extra beef stock, if preferred
1 teaspoon **dried oregano**
125 g (4 oz) **dried lasagne
  sheets**
salt and **pepper**

Topping
250 g (8 oz) **mascarpone
  cheese**
2 **eggs**
4 tablespoons freshly grated
  Parmesan cheese

Preheat the slow cooker if necessary; see the manufacturer's instructions. Heat the oil in a large frying pan, add the mince and onion and fry, covered, for 10 minutes, stirring from time to time, until browned.

Add the peppers, mushrooms, celery and garlic and fry for a further 5 minutes, stirring more frequently.

Mix in the passata, stock and wine, if using, then the dried herbs, and season with salt and pepper to taste. Bring to the boil, stirring.

Spoon one-quarter of the mince mixture into the base of the slow cooker pot. Cover with one-third of the lasagne sheets, breaking them into large pieces so that they fit in a single layer. Continue layering in this way, ending with a layer of mince.

Cover with the lid and cook on low for 4–5 hours until the beef and vegetables are tender. Whisk the mascarpone, eggs and a little salt and pepper together until smooth. Spoon the mixture over the top of the lasagne, spreading it out into an even layer. Sprinkle with the Parmesan, then re-cover and cook for 1–1¼ hours or until the topping is just set.

Lift the slow cooker pot out of the machine with oven gloves, then brown the lasagne under a preheated grill. Spoon into shallow bowls and serve with salad, if liked.

For beef moussaka, make up the meaty base as above, omitting the lasagne sheets and layering with 2 sliced and fried aubergines. Cook on low as above, then top with the mascarpone topping and cook until set. Grill, if liked, then serve as above.

easy lamb & barley risotto

Preparation time **10 minutes**
Cooking temperature **low**
Cooking time **7–8 hours**
Serves **4**

20 g (¾ oz) **mixed dried
mushrooms**
1 litre (1¾ pint) **boiling
vegetable stock**
4 tablespoons **cream sherry**
or **fresh orange juice**
1 **onion**, finely chopped
1 teaspoon **ground cumin**
2 **garlic cloves**, finely chopped
40 g (1½ oz) **sultanas**
125 g (4 oz) **pearl barley**
4 **lamb chump chops**, about
150 g (5 oz) each
250 g (8 oz) **ready-prepared
pumpkin** or **butternut
squash**, cut into 2 cm
(¾ inch) dice
salt and **pepper**
chopped **mint** and **parsley**,
to garnish

Preheat the slow cooker if necessary; see the manufacturer's instructions. Add the dried mushrooms to the slow cooker pot, pour in the boiling stock, then stir in the sherry or orange juice, onion, cumin, garlic and sultanas. Spoon in the barley and season with salt and pepper.

Arrange the chops on top in a single layer, season, then tuck the pumpkin or squash into the gaps between the chops. Press the chops and squash down lightly into the stock, then cover with the lid and cook on low for 7–8 hours until the lamb and vegetables are tender.

Lift the chops out of the slow cooker, stir the barley, then spoon on to plates, top with the chops, broken into pieces, and sprinkle with the herbs. Serve with spoonfuls of harissa, if liked.

For pumpkin & barley risotto, omit the lamb and use 400 g (13 oz) diced pumpkin. Cook as above, then add 125 g (4 oz) spinach to the risotto for the last 15 minutes of cooking. Serve topped with spoonfuls of Greek yogurt, chopped fresh mint and parsley and buttery fried flaked almonds.

pot roast lamb with za'atar rub

Preparation time **20 minutes**
Cooking temperature **high**
Cooking time **5–6 hours**
Serves **4**

1 tablespoon **extra virgin olive oil**
2 **onions**, thinly sliced
2 **garlic cloves**, finely chopped
250 ml (8 fl oz) **lamb stock**
1 tablespoon **tomato purée**
2 teaspoons **za'atar spice mix**
200 ml (7 fl oz) **dry white wine** or extra **lamb stock**, if preferred
1 tablespoon **cornflour**
400 g (13 oz) **new potatoes**, scrubbed and thickly sliced
½ **boneless lamb shoulder**, about 750 g (1½ lb)
salt and **pepper**
chopped **parsley** and **mint**, to garnish

To serve
2 **courgettes**, thinly sliced
1 tablespoon **olive oil**
½ teaspoon **za'atar spice mix**
400 g (13 oz) **hummus**

Preheat the slow cooker if necessary; see the manufacturer's instructions. Heat the oil in a large frying pan, add the onions and fry for 5 minutes until softened and just beginning to brown. Stir in the garlic, stock, tomato purée and half the za'atar. Pour in the wine, if using,keeping back about 2 tablespoons of wine or stock.

Stir the cornflour into the remaining wine until smooth, then add to the frying pan. Bring to the boil, stirring.

Add the potatoes to the base of the slow cooker pot, then pour in the hot stock mixture. Remove the strings from the lamb, open it out flat and rub with the reserved za'atar and season with salt and pepper. Add to the slow cooker pot and press the meat beneath the liquid. Cover with the lid and cook on high for 5–6 hours or until the lamb is almost falling apart.

Toss the sliced courgettes with the oil, za'atar and a little salt and pepper. Cook over a preheated griddle pan until lightly browned and tender. Divide the hummus between 4 plates, spread into an even layer and make a thin ridge around the sides to contain the lamb sauce. Break the lamb into pieces, then spoon it on to the hummus with the sauce. Add the courgettes and sprinkle with chopped parsley and mint.

For pot roast lamb with rosemary, add 200 ml (7 fl oz) red wine in place of the white wine, if using, in the sauce, plus 2 tablespoons redcurrant jelly and 3 sprigs of rosemary. Mix the cornflour with the reserved wine or stock as above. Add the potatoes and plain lamb joint to the slow cooker, then pour over the hot stock mixture. Cook as above and serve with mixed steamed vegetables.

easy cheats

salmon tikka salad

Preparation time **20 minutes**
Cooking temperature **low**
Cooking time **1¾–2 hours**
Serves **4**

4 **salmon fillets**, about 125 g
   (4 oz) each
1 tablespoon **tikka masala
   curry paste**
small handful of **coriander**,
   roughly chopped
juice of 1 **lemon**
150 ml (¼ pint) **boiling
   fish stock**
salt and **pepper**

To serve
2 **little gem lettuces**
small handful of **coriander**
½ **cucumber,** thinly sliced
100 g (3½ oz) **radishes**,
   trimmed and thinly sliced
150 g (5 oz) **natural yogurt**
½ **red onion**, thinly sliced

Preheat the slow cooker if necessary; see the manufacturer's instructions. Arrange the salmon in a single layer over the base of the slow cooker pot. Spread the top of the salmon with the curry paste, then sprinkle over the chopped coriander and lemon juice.

Pour over the boiling stock, season with a little salt and pepper, then cover with the lid. Cook on low for 1¾–2 hours or until the salmon is cooked through and flakes easily.

When the salmon is ready, thickly slice the lettuce and arrange over serving plates with a few coriander leaves. Finely chop the remaining coriander and place it in a bowl with the cucumber, radishes and yogurt. Season with salt and pepper and toss together. Spoon the mixture over the lettuce.

Lift the salmon out of the slow cooker with a slotted spoon, break into pieces, discarding any skin and bones, and spoon over the salad. Sprinkle with the red onion and serve immediately.

For harissa salmon salad, spread the salmon with 1 tablespoon harissa paste, then cook and serve as above.

mexican baked beans

Preparation time **15 minutes**
Cooking temperature **low**
Cooking time **8–9 hours**
Serves **4**

250 g (8 oz) **ready-diced
  carrot and swede**
2 x 300 g (10 oz) cans **hot
  and spicy mixed beans**
500 g (1 lb) **tomatoes**,
  skinned, if liked, roughly
  chopped
2 **garlic cloves,** finely chopped
  (optional)
1 teaspoon **dried oregano**
8 large **soft tortilla wraps,**
  to serve

Preheat the slow cooker if necessary; see the manufacturer's instructions. Add the diced carrot and swede to the base of the slow cooker pot. Pour over the canned beans and their sauce, add the tomatoes, garlic, if using, and the oregano and stir together.

Cover with the lid and cook on low for 8–9 hours until the vegetables are tender.

When ready to serve, warm the tortillas according to the packet instructions. Spoon the spicy beans into bowls and serve with tortillas and spoonfuls of crème fraîche and grated cheese, if liked.

For Mexican baked beans & gammon, trim the fat from 1 large gammon steak and dice the steak, then add the gammon to the slow cooker with the other ingredients. Cook and serve as above.

green bean risotto with pesto

Preparation time **20 minutes**
Cooking temperature **low**
Cooking time **2 hours**
5 minutes—2½ hours
Serves **4**

25 g (1 oz) **butter**
1 tablespoon **olive oil**
1 **onion**, chopped
2 **garlic cloves**, chopped
250 g (8 oz) **risotto rice**
1.25 litres (2¼ pints) **boiling vegetable stock**
2 teaspoons **pesto**
125 g (4 oz) **extra fine frozen green beans**
125 g (4 oz) **frozen peas**
salt and **pepper**

To garnish
Parmesan shavings
basil leaves

Preheat the slow cooker if necessary; see the manufacturer's instructions. Heat the butter and oil in a saucepan, add the onion and fry, stirring, for 5 minutes or until softened and just beginning to brown.

Stir in the garlic and rice and cook for 1 minute. Add all but 150 ml (¼ pint) of the stock, season with salt and pepper, then bring to the boil. Transfer to the slow cooker pot, cover with the lid and cook on low for 1¾–2 hours until the rice is tender.

Stir in the pesto and the remaining stock if more liquid is needed. Place the frozen vegetables on top of the rice, re-cover and cook for a further 20–30 minutes or until the vegetables are cooked through. Serve garnished with Parmesan shavings and basil leaves.

For green bean risotto with sage & pancetta, add 75 g (3 oz) diced pancetta or smoked streaky bacon when frying the chopped onion. Add 2 sprigs of sage to the mixture when adding the stock instead of the pesto. Replace the basil leaves with some small sage leaves.

mixed vegetable balti

Preparation time **20 minutes**
Cooking temperature **low**
Cooking time **5–6 hours**
Serves **4**

1 small **cauliflower**, cut
  into florets
375 g (12 oz) **sweet potato**,
  cut into 2 cm (¾ inch) cubes
1 **red pepper**, cored, deseeded
  and cut into chunks
100 g (3½ oz) **green beans**,
  each cut into 3
450 g (14½ oz) jar **balti
  sauce**

To serve
1 tablespoon **olive oil**
1 **onion**, thinly sliced
handful of chopped **coriander
  leaves**
1 teaspoon **brown mustard
  seeds**
150 g (5 oz) **Greek yogurt**
naan breads

Preheat the slow cooker if necessary; see the manufacturer's instructions. Add the cauliflower, sweet potato, red pepper and beans to the slow cooker pot.

Pour the curry sauce into a saucepan and bring to the boil, or microwave if preferred. Pour the sauce over the vegetables, cover and cook on low for 5–6 hours or until the vegetables are just tender. Stir halfway through the cooking time and again at the end.

When ready to serve, heat the oil in a frying pan, add the onion and chopped coriander and fry for 4–5 minutes until softened and browned. Mix in the mustard seeds and cook for a further 1–2 minutes more.

Spoon the curry into bowls, top with spoonfuls of the yogurt and the fried onion mixture. Serve with warmed naan breads.

For chicken & vegetable balti, omit the cauliflower and replace with 600 g (1 lb 3½ oz) boneless, skinless diced chicken thighs. Add the remaining vegetables and hot sauce and cook on low for 8–9 hours until the chicken is cooked through and the vegetables are tender. Serve as above.

red pepper & chorizo tortilla

Preparation time **20 minutes**
Cooking temperature **high**
Cooking time **2–2½ hours**
Serves **4**

1 tablespoon **olive oil**, plus
  extra for greasing
1 small **onion**, chopped
75 g (3 oz) **chorizo**, diced
6 **eggs**
150 ml (¼ pint) **milk**
100 g (3½ oz) **roasted red
  peppers from a jar**, sliced
250 g (8 oz) cooked **potatoes**,
  sliced
salt and **pepper**

Preheat the slow cooker if necessary. Lightly oil a
1.2 litre (2 pint) ovenproof soufflé dish and line the base
with nonstick baking paper. Heat the oil in a small frying
pan over a medium heat, add the onion and chorizo and
cook for 4–5 minutes until the onion has softened.

Beat the eggs and milk together in a mixing bowl and
season to taste. Add the onion and chorizo, red peppers
and potatoes and toss together.

Tip the mixture into the oiled dish, cover the top with foil
and put in the slow cooker pot. Pour boiling water into
the slow cooker pot to come halfway up the sides of the
dish, cover and cook on high for 2–2½ hours until the
egg mixture has just set in the centre.

Loosen the edges of the tortilla with a round-bladed
knife, turn it out on to a plate and peel off the lining paper.
Cut into slices and serve hot or cold with salad, if liked.

For cheesy bacon & rosemary tortilla, follow the
recipe above, using 75 g (3 oz) diced smoked streaky
bacon instead of the chorizo. Beat the eggs and milk in
a bowl with the chopped leaves from 2 small rosemary
sprigs, 4 tablespoons freshly grated Parmesan
or Cheddar cheese and 75 g (3 oz) sliced button
mushrooms. Season to taste and continue as above.

pork with black bean sauce

Preparation time **20 minutes**,
  plus overnight marinating
Cooking temperature **high**
  and **low**
Cooking time **8–10 hours**
Serves **4**

4 **spare rib pork steaks**,
  about 175 g (6 oz) each
2 tablespoons **cornflour**
4 tablespoons **soy sauce**
4 cm (1½ inch) piece of
  fresh root ginger, peeled
  and finely chopped
2 **garlic cloves**, finely chopped
100 g (3½ oz) **black bean
  sauce**
300 ml (½ pint) **boiling
  chicken stock**
chopped **coriander leaves**,
  to garnish
pepper

To serve
1 tablespoon **sunflower oil**
300 g (10 oz) **mixed
  vegetable stir-fry**
rice

Put the pork steaks into a shallow non-metallic dish.
Put the cornflour and soy sauce in a small bowl and
mix to a smooth paste, then add the ginger, garlic, black
bean sauce and a little pepper. Pour over the pork, cover
with clingfilm and marinate in the refrigerator overnight.

Preheat the slow cooker if necessary; see the
manufacturer's instructions. Put the pork and marinade
into the slow cooker pot. Pour over the boiling stock,
cover with the lid and cook on high for 30 minutes.
Reduce the heat and cook on low for 7½–9½ hours
or set to auto for 8–10 hours until the pork is tender.

When almost ready to serve, heat the oil in a large
frying pan, add the mixed vegetables and stir-fry for
2–3 minutes or until just tender. Spoon the pork on
to plates lined with rice and top with the vegetables.

For sweet & sour pork, omit the black bean sauce
from the marinade, add the marinated pork to the
slow cooker pot with 1 bunch of sliced spring onions,
1 cored, deseeded and sliced red pepper and 100 g
(3½ oz) sliced mushrooms. Replace the chicken stock
with a 425 g (14 oz) jar sweet and sour sauce. Bring
the sauce to the boil in a saucepan or the microwave,
then pour into the slow cooker pot. Continue as above.

cheat's fish pie

Preparation time **20 minutes**
Cooking temperature **low**
Cooking time **2½–3 hours**
Serves **4**

625 g (1¼ lb) **cubed fish pie mix** (with salmon, white and smoked fish)
4 **spring onions**, thinly sliced
500 g (1 lb) chilled carton **cheese sauce**
few drops of **Tabasco sauce**
250 g (8 oz) **frozen peas**
500 g (1 lb) chilled pack **buttery mashed potato**
50 g (2 oz) **mature Cheddar cheese**, grated

Preheat the slow cooker if necessary, see manufacturer's instructions. Add the cubed fish to the base of the slow cooker pot, then add the spring onions, cheese sauce and a few drops of Tabasco and gently stir together. Level the surface, pressing the fish beneath the sauce.

Cover and cook on low for 2½–3 hours or until the fish is cooked and the sauce is piping hot.

When the fish is cooked, add the peas to a saucepan of boiling water, cook for 3–4 minutes, then drain and mash. Heat the mashed potato in the microwave according to the packet instructions then mix in the peas.

Spoon the fish mixture into a large ovenproof pie dish, spoon the mash on top, then sprinkle with the grated cheese. Cook under a preheated medium grill until browned. Serve immediately.

For cheat's fish pasta bake, cook the fish in the sauce as above. Cook 200 g (7 oz) dried pasta twists in a saucepan of boiling water for 5 minutes, then add the frozen peas and cook for 4–5 minutes until the peas are hot and the pasta is tender. Drain, then stir into the sauce and spoon into a large shallow dish. Sprinkle with the grated Cheddar cheese and 2 tablespoons fresh breadcrumbs. Grill for 5 minutes until the top is crisp and golden.

peasant paella

Preparation time **20 minutes**
Cooking temperature **high**
Cooking time **4¾–6 hours**
Serves **4**

1 tablespoon **olive oil**
500 g (1 lb) **boneless, skinless chicken thighs**, cubed
1 **onion**, chopped
60 g (2¼ oz) **chorizo**, sliced
2 **garlic cloves**, finely chopped
1 **red pepper**, cored, deseeded and diced
1 **orange pepper**, cored, deseeded and diced
2 **celery sticks**, diced
2 pinches of **saffron threads**
½ teaspoon **dried Mediterranean herbs**
750 ml (1¼ pints) **boiling chicken stock**
175 g (6 oz) **long-grain brown rice**
125 g (4 oz) **frozen peas**
salt and **pepper**
2 tablespoons chopped **parsley**, to garnish

Preheat the slow cooker if necessary; see the manufacturer's instructions. Heat the oil in a large frying pan over a high heat until hot. Add the chicken, a few pieces at a time, until all the chicken is in the pan, then cook for 5 minutes, stirring, until browned. Use a slotted spoon to transfer the chicken to the slow cooker pot.

Add the onion, chorizo and garlic to the frying pan and cook for 3–4 minutes, stirring, until the onion begins to colour. Add the peppers and celery, stir well, then transfer to the slow cooker pot. Mix the saffron and dried herbs with the boiling stock, season to taste, then pour into the slow cooker pot and stir well. Cover and cook on high for 3–4 hours.

Place the rice in a sieve and rinse under cold running water, then stir into the chicken mixture. Re-cover and cook for 1½–1¾ hours until the rice is tender and the chicken is cooked through. Stir in the peas and continue cooking for 15 minutes. Serve garnished with chopped parsley.

For seafood paella, follow the recipe, omitting the chicken. Defrost a 400 g (13 oz) pack frozen mixed seafood and pat dry on kitchen paper. Heat 1 tablespoon olive oil in a large frying pan, add the seafood and fry for 4–5 minutes until it is piping hot. Stir into the finished paella and garnish with the parsley.

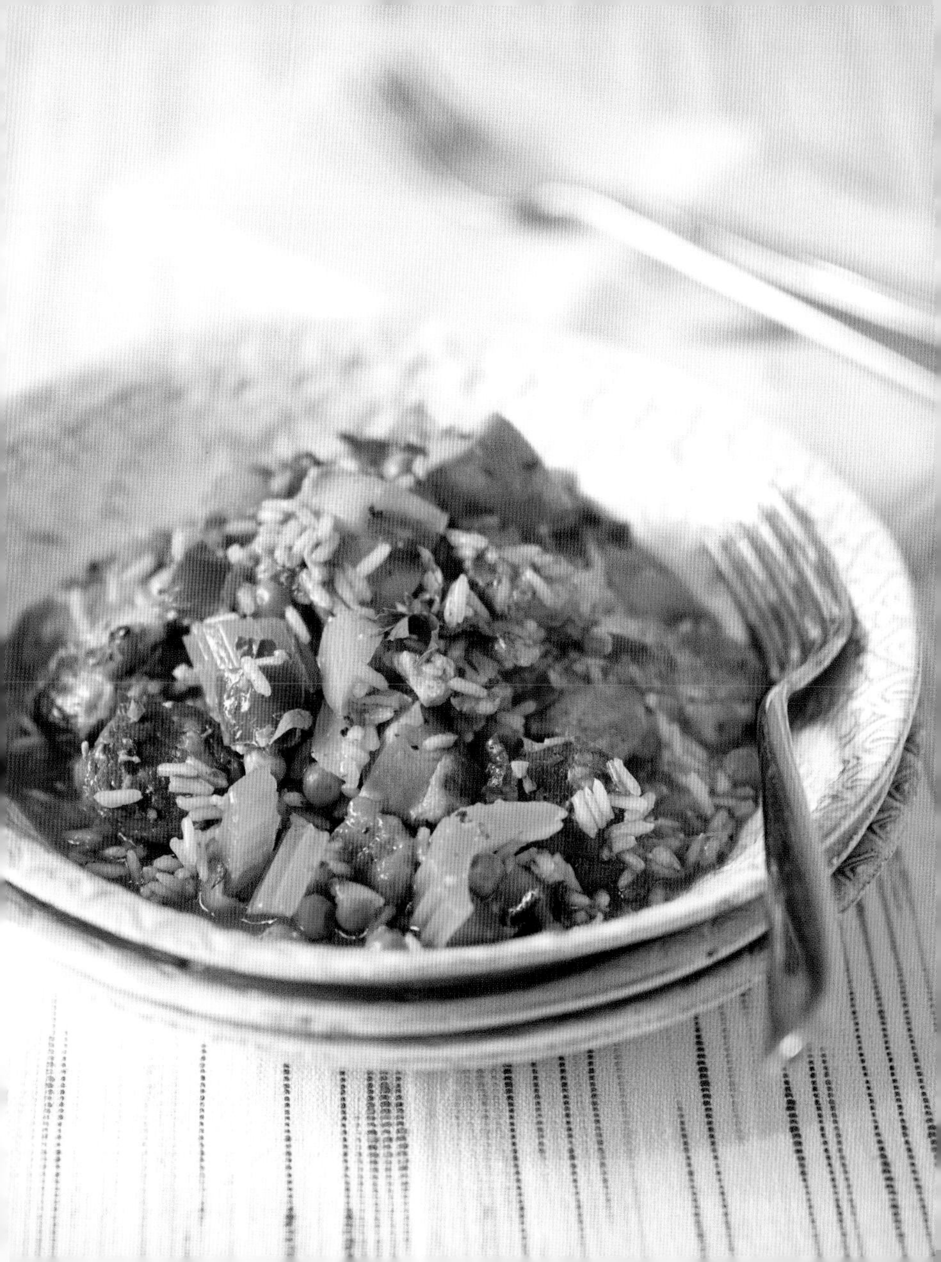

chinese lemon chicken

Preparation time **15 minutes**
Cooking temperature **low**
Cooking time **8–9 hours**
Serves **4**

625 g (1 ¼ lb) **boneless,
  skinless chicken thighs**,
  cubed
4 **spring onions**, sliced
500 g (1 lb) jar **Peking
  lemon sauce**
1 tablespoon **sunflower oil**
300 g (10 oz) pack **oriental
  stir-fry vegetables with
  sliced bamboo shoots
  and water chestnuts**
juice of **1 lemon**
rice, to serve

Preheat the slow cooker if necessary; see the
manufacturer's instructions. Add the chicken and spring
onions to the slow cooker pot.

Bring the sauce to the boil in a saucepan or in a bowl
in the microwave. Pour the sauce over the chicken in
the slow cooker pot, then cover with the lid and cook on
low for 8–9 hours until the chicken is cooked through.

When ready to serve, heat the oil in a frying pan, add
the stir-fry vegetables and cook for 2–3 minutes until
piping hot. Stir the lemon juice into the chicken, then
spoon it into rice-lined bowls and top with the stir-fried
vegetables. Garnish with lemon rind curls, if liked.

For Chinese lemon salmon, add 4 salmon pieces,
about 125 g (4 oz) each, to the base of the slow cooker
pot with the spring onions instead of the chicken.
Continue as the recipe above, but cook on low for
1 ½–1 ¾ hours, then top with the stir-fried vegetables.

chicken ratatouille

Preparation time **15 minutes**
Cooking temperature **low**
Cooking time **8–9 hours**
Serves **4**

625 g (1 ¼ lb) **boneless, skinless chicken thighs**, halved
4 **smoked streaky bacon rashers**, diced
500 g (1 lb) **frozen chargrilled Mediterranean vegetables**
200 g (7 oz) canned **chopped tomatoes**
300 ml (½ pint) **water**
35 g (1 ½ oz) sachet **powdered chicken in red wine sauce for slow cookers**
2 **garlic cloves**, finely chopped
basil leaves, to garnish

Preheat the slow cooker if necessary; see the manufacturer's instructions. Add the chicken and bacon to the slow cooker pot, then scatter the frozen vegetables on top.

Add the tomatoes, measurement water, sauce mix and garlic to a saucepan and bring to the boil, stirring until smooth. Pour the mixture over the chicken, then cover with the lid and cook on low for 8–9 hours until the chicken is cooked through.

Garnish with basil leaves and serve with flatbreads, if liked.

For spicy sausage ratatouille, omit the chicken and add 300 g (10 oz) Kabanos polish sausage, thickly sliced, to the slow cooker pot with the bacon and remaining ingredients. Cook as above.

turkey, leek & cranberry pies

Preparation time **25 minutes**, plus **20 minutes** in a conventional oven
Cooking temperature **low**
Cooking time **8–9 hours**
Serves **4**

500 g (1 lb) **turkey breast slices**, cubed
1 **leek**, thinly sliced
150 g (5 oz) **button mushrooms**, sliced
400 g (13 oz) can **red wine cooking sauce** or **tomato-based pasta sauce**
150 ml (¼ pint) **water**
juice of ½ **orange**
2 tablespoons **cranberry sauce**
320 g (11 oz) **chilled ready-rolled, all-butter puff pastry**
beaten egg, to glaze

Preheat the slow cooker if necessary; see the manufacturer's instructions. Add the turkey, leek and mushrooms to the slow cooker pot.

Pour the cooking sauce, measurement water and orange juice into a saucepan and add the cranberry sauce. Bring to the boil, stirring. Alternatively, heat the mixture in a microwave. Pour the liquid into the slow cooker pot, press the turkey beneath the surface of the sauce, then cover with the lid and cook on low for 8–9 hours until the turkey is cooked through.

Spoon the turkey mixture into 4 individual round 300 ml (½ pint) pie dishes, each about 10 cm (4 inches) in diameter. Unroll the pastry, cut out 4 round pastry lids, using the dishes as a size guide, and stick 1 lid on to the rim of each dish with a little beaten egg to cover the turkey mixture. Brush the pastry tops with beaten egg and decorate with shapes cut from the trimmings.

Bake in a preheated oven, 200°C (400°F), Gas Mark 6, for 15–20 minutes until the pastry is puffed and golden. Serve with broccoli and green beans, if liked.

For garlicky lamb, leek & cranberry pies, omit the turkey and replace with 600 g (1 lb 3½ oz) diced lamb fillet and 2 finely chopped garlic cloves. Add the remaining ingredients, cook and serve as above.

beef & ale stew with herb dumplings

Preparation time **20 minutes**
Cooking temperature **low
and high**
Cooking time **8½–9 hours
40 minutes**
Serves **4**

750 g (1 ½ lb) **lean stewing
beef**, cubed
250 g (8 oz) **ready-diced
carrot and swede**
1 **leek**, thickly sliced
2 **portobello mushrooms**,
sliced
500 g (1 lb) jar **beef and ale
cooking sauce** or can
beef soup
150 ml (¼ pint) **beef stock**
142 g (4½ oz) pack **herby
dumpling mix**
small handful of **parsley**,
finely chopped

Preheat the slow cooker if necessary; see
manufacturer's instructions. Add the beef to the slow
cooker pot, sprinkle over the diced carrot and swede
and the leek and mushrooms, then mix together.

Pour the sauce and stock into a saucepan, bring to the
boil, stirring, then pour the mixture over the meat in the
slow cooker pot. Press the raw ingredients beneath
the surface of the liquid. Cover with the lid and cook
on low for 8–9 hours until the beef is tender.

Make the dumplings. Mix the dumpling mix and
chopped parsley with cold water and chopped parsley
according to the packet instructions to make a soft
dough. Cut the dough into 12 equal pieces and shape
them into small balls.

Stir the casserole, place the dumplings on top in a
single layer, leaving small spaces between them, then
cook on high for 30–40 minutes or until the dumplings
are light and fluffy. Spoon into shallow bowls to serve.

For sausage & ale stew with parsley dumplings,

grill 8 large sausages until browned but not cooked
through, then add them to the slow cooker pot with the
vegetables and hot sauce-and-stock mix. Cook and
serve as above.

thai beef curry

Preparation time **15 minutes**
Cooking temperature **low**
Cooking time **8 hours**
 5 minutes–10 hours
 10 minutes
Serves **4**

400 ml (14 fl oz) can **full-fat
 coconut milk**
1 bunch of **spring onions**,
 very finely chopped
3 tablespoons **laksa Thai
 curry paste**
3 **dried kaffir lime leaves**
2 tablespoons **palm sugar**
 or **light muscovado sugar**
2 tablespoons **rice vinegar**
2 teaspoons **fish sauce**
750 g (1½ lb) **lean braising
 beef**, cubed
100 g (3½ oz) **mangetout**,
 cut in half on the diagonal

To serve
small handful of **coriander**,
 torn into pieces
sliced **red chilli**
lime wedges

Preheat the slow cooker if necessary; see the manufacturer's instructions. Pour the coconut milk into a saucepan, add the spring onions, laksa paste and lime leaves, then add the sugar, vinegar and fish sauce. Bring to the boil, stirring.

Place the beef on the base of the slow cooker pot, pour over the hot coconut broth, stir together, then press the beef beneath the surface of the liquid. Cover with the lid and cook on low for 8–10 hours until the beef is tender.

Stir the curry, sprinkle the mangetout over the top, then re-cover and cook for 5–10 minutes until the mangetout is hot yet still crunchy. Ladle the curry into rice-lined bowls, if liked, and sprinkle with the coriander and chilli. Squeeze lime juice over to taste.

For Thai pumpkin & mushroom curry, omit the braising beef and add 500 g (1 lb) ready-prepared pumpkin or butternut squash cut into 2 cm (¾ inch) cubes and 200 g (7 oz) halved cup mushrooms. Cook with the hot coconut broth on low for 7–8 hours until the vegetables are tender, then serve as above.

lamb ragù

Preparation time **15 minutes**
Cooking temperature **low**
Cooking time **8–9 hours**
Serves **4**

650 g (1 lb 5 oz) jar **tomato
  and pepper ragù sauce**
125 ml (4 fl oz) **red wine** or
  lamb stock
300 g (10 oz) scrubbed **baby
  new potatoes**, thickly sliced
600 g (1 lb 3½ oz) **lamb,**
  diced
1 **red pepper**, cored,
  deseeded and cut into
  chunks
1 **yellow pepper**, cored,
  deseeded and cut into
  chunks

Preheat the slow cooker if necessary; see the
manufacturer's instructions. Pour the ragù sauce
and wine or stock into a saucepan and bring to the
boil. Alternatively, heat the mixture in a microwave.

Place the potato slices on the base of the slow cooker
pot, arrange the lamb on top, then add the red and
yellow peppers. Pour over the hot sauce, then cover
with the lid and cook on low for 8–9 hours until the
potatoes and lamb are tender.

Stir the ragu. Serve garnished with basil leaves and
accompanied by warm garlic bread, if liked.

For beef & mushroom ragù, make up the recipe as
above adding 600 g (1 lb 3½ oz) diced beef instead
of the lamb and 150 g (5 oz) sliced cup mushrooms
in place of the yellow pepper.

food to
impress

baked red onions & herb couscous

Preparation time **25 minutes**
Cooking temperature **high**
Cooking time **4–5 hours**
Serves **4**

4 large **red onions**, peeled
250 g (8 oz) **minced beef**
1 teaspoon **ground cinnamon**
1 teaspoon **ground cumin**
1 teaspoon **turmeric**
2 tablespoons **currants**
400 g (13 oz) can **chopped tomatoes**
125 ml (4 fl oz) **vegetable stock**
2 **garlic cloves**, finely chopped
2 teaspoons **light muscovado sugar**
salt and **pepper**

Herb couscous
200 g (7 oz) **couscous**
400 ml (14 fl oz) **boiling water**
2 tablespoons **olive oil**
handful of **parsley**, chopped
handful of **coriander**, chopped

Preheat the slow cooker if necessary; see the manufacturer's instructions. Cut a thin slice off the top of each onion and reserve. Hollow out the centre of 1 onion to make a cup, then repeat with the other onions. (Save the scooped-out onion to use in other recipes.)

Put the minced beef in a bowl and stir in half the ground spices, then add the currants and a little salt and pepper and mix together. Spoon into the onion cups, then top with the reserved onion lids.

Heat the tomatoes, stock, garlic and sugar with the remaining spices. Pour into the base of the slow cooker pot, then add the onions. Cover with the lid and cook on high for 4–5 hours until the onions are tender.

Soak the couscous in the boiling water for 5 minutes. Add the oil, herbs and a little salt and pepper and fluff up with a fork. Spoon on to plates, top with the onions and serve with the sauce alongside.

For baked red peppers with herby couscous,
halve 2 red peppers and scoop out the cores and seeds. Fill with the mince mixture, then arrange on top of the tomato mixture. Cook and serve as above.

vegetable biryani

Preparation time **25 minutes**
Cooking temperature **low**
Cooking time **4½–5½ hours**
Serves **4**

25 g (1 oz) **butter**
1 tablespoon **sunflower oil**
1 **onion**, chopped
1 **aubergine**, diced
2 tablespoons **mild curry paste**
2.5 cm (1 inch) piece of **fresh
  root ginger**, peeled and
  finely chopped
2 **garlic cloves**, finely chopped
125 g (4 oz) **green beans**,
  each trimmed and cut into 3
125 g (4 oz) **frozen peas**
150 g (5 oz) **cherry tomatoes**,
  halved
200 g (7 oz) **easy-cook
  long-grain white rice**
3 **cardamom pods**, crushed
1 litre (1¾ pints) **boiling
  vegetable stock**
salt and **pepper**
handful of **coriander**, torn into
  pieces, to garnish

To serve
25 g (1 oz) **butter**
25 g (1 oz) **flaked almonds**
50 g (2 oz) **cashew nuts**

Preheat the slow cooker if necessary; see the manufacturer's instructions. Heat the butter and oil in a large frying pan, add the onion and aubergine and fry for 5 minutes, stirring, until both are lightly browned.

Mix in the curry paste, ginger and garlic, then add the beans, peas and tomatoes and season to taste.

Sprinkle half the rice over the base of the slow cooker pot, spoon over the vegetable mix, then cover with the remaining rice, tucking the cardamom pods and their black seeds into the rice. Pour over the boiling stock, then cover with the lid and cook on low for 4½–5½ hours until the rice is tender.

Heat the butter in a frying pan, add the nuts and fry for 2–3 minutes, stirring, until golden. Spoon the biryani on to plates, sprinkle the nuts on top and serve garnished with coriander.

For salmon biryani, omit the aubergine and add the remaining vegetables to the fried onion. Sprinkle half the rice into the slow cooker pot and arrange 4 x 125 g (4 oz) pieces of salmon on top. Spoon over the onion mix, then the remaining rice. Add the stock, then cook and serve as above.

aubergine timbale

Preparation time **25 minutes**
Cooking temperature **high**
Cooking time **1½–2 hours**
Serves **2**

4 tablespoons **olive oil**, plus
  extra for greasing
1 large **aubergine**, thinly sliced
1 small **onion**, chopped
1 **garlic clove**, finely chopped
½ teaspoon **ground
  cinnamon**
¼ teaspoon **grated nutmeg**
25 g (1 oz) **pistachio nuts**,
  roughly chopped
25 g (1 oz) **pitted dates**,
  roughly chopped
25 g (1 oz) **ready-to-eat dried
  apricots**, roughly chopped
75 g (3 oz) **easy-cook
  long-grain rice**
300 ml (½ pint) **boiling
  vegetable stock**
salt and **pepper**

Preheat the slow cooker if necessary; see the manufacturer's instructions. Check that 2 soufflé dishes, each 350 ml (12 fl oz), will fit in the slow cooker pot. Oil the bases and line them with nonstick baking paper.

Heat 1 tablespoon of the oil in a large frying pan, add one-third of the aubergines and fry on both sides until softened and golden. Transfer the aubergine slices to a plate. Repeat with the remaining aubergines slices using 2 more tablespoonfuls of the oil.

Heat the remaining oil in the pan, add the onion and fry for 5 minutes or until soft. Stir in the garlic, spices, nuts, fruit and rice. Season and and mix well.

Arrange one-third of the aubergine slices in the bases of the 2 dishes, overlapping the slices. Spoon one-quarter of the rice mixture into each dish, add a second layer of aubergine slices, then divide the remaining rice equally between the dishes. Top with the remaining aubergine slices. Pour the stock into the dishes, cover with lightly oiled foil and put in the slow cooker pot.

Pour boiling water into the pot to come halfway up the sides of the dishes. Cover with the lid and cook on high for 1½–2 hours or until the rice is tender. Lift the dishes out of the slow cooker pot using oven gloves and remove the foil. Loosen the edges of the timbales with a knife, turn out on to plates and peel off the lining paper. Serve hot with rocket leaves and baked tomatoes, if liked.

For curried aubergine timbale, omit the cinnamon and nutmeg and replace with 1 tablespoon mild curry paste. Continue as above. Serve with a creamy spinach side dish.

tomato, pepper & garlic bruschetta

Preparation time **20 minutes**
Cooking temperature **high**
Cooking time **3–5 hours**
Serves **4**

1 large **red pepper**, quartered,
   cored and deseeded
500 g (1 lb) **plum tomatoes**,
   halved
4 large **garlic cloves**, unpeeled
leaves from 2–3 **thyme sprigs**
1 teaspoon **caster sugar**
1 tablespoon **extra virgin
   olive oil**

To serve
8 slices of **French bread**,
   175 g (6 oz) in total
8 **pitted black olives in brine**,
   drained
salt and **pepper**

Preheat the slow cooker if necessary; see the manufacturer's instructions. Arrange the pepper pieces, skin-side down, in the base of the slow cooker pot, arrange the tomatoes on top, then tuck the garlic in among them. Scatter the thyme leaves on top, reserving a little to garnish. Sprinkle with the sugar and drizzle with the oil.

Season to taste, cover and cook on high for 3–5 hours until the vegetables are tender but the tomatoes still hold their shape.

Lift the vegetables out of the slow cooker pot with a slotted spoon. Peel the skins off the peppers, tomatoes and garlic, then roughly chop the vegetables and toss together. Adjust the seasoning if necessary.

Toast the bread on both sides, then arrange on a serving plate. Spoon the tomato mixture on top. Arrange the olives and reserved thyme on the bruschetta and serve as a light lunch or starter.

For quick tomato & pepper pizzas, follow the recipe above to cook the tomato and pepper mixture, then spoon it on to 2 halved and toasted ciabatta rolls. Sprinkle with 50 g (2 oz) grated Cheddar cheese and place under a preheated hot grill until the cheese is melted. Serve with salad.

seafood laksa

Preparation time **20 minutes**
Cooking temperature **low**
Cooking time **2¼–2½ hours**
Serves **4**

1 bunch of **spring onions**
2 **green finger chillies**
2.5 cm (1 inch) piece of **fresh root ginger**, peeled and sliced
2 **garlic cloves**, sliced
2 handfuls of **coriander**, roughly torn
2 tablespoons **sunflower oil**
400 ml (14 fl oz) can **full-fat coconut milk**
200 ml (7 fl oz) **fish stock**
2 teaspoons **palm sugar**
2 teaspoons **tamarind paste**
2 teaspoons **fish sauce**
½ teaspoon **turmeric**
2 **dried kaffir lime leaves**
300 g (10 oz) **cod fillet**
300 g (10 oz) **salmon fillet**
175 g (6 oz) **cooked peeled prawns**, rinsed and drained
300 g (10 oz) **bean sprouts**, rinsed and drained
375 g (12 oz) pack chilled **ready-cooked fine rice noodles**
¼ **cucumber**, cut into thin shreds

Preheat the slow cooker if necessary; see the manufacturer's instructions. Trim and quarter the spring onions. Halve the chillies lengthways and remove the seeds. Finely chop the onions, chilli, garlic and half the coriander in a food processor if using or with a large knife.

Heat half of the oil in a frying pan, add the chopped onion mix and fry over a low heat for 3–4 minutes until just softened. Stir in the coconut milk, stock, sugar, tamarind paste and fish sauce, then mix in the turmeric and kaffir lime leaves. Bring to the boil, stirring.

Halve and skin the fish fillets and arrange them snugly together in the base of the slow cooker pot in a single layer. Pour over the hot coconut broth, then cover with the lid and cook on low for 2–2¼ hours until the fish is cooked through.

Break the fish into large pieces and add the prawns. Cover and cook for 15 minutes until the prawns are piping hot. Meanwhile, heat the remaining oil in a wok or large frying pan, add the bean sprouts and noodles and stir-fry for 2–3 minutes. Spoon into the bases of large shallow serving bowls.

Ladle the fish and broth into the bowls, then garnish with the remaining coriander and the shreds of cucumber. Serve immediately.

For beef laksa, add vegetable stock in place of the fish stock and 625 g (1¼ lb) trimmed and thinly sliced rump steak instead of the cod, salmon and prawns. Cook and serve as above.

three-fish gratin

Preparation time **20 minutes**
Cooking temperature **low**
Cooking time **2–3 hours**
Serves **4**

2 tablespoons **cornflour**
400 ml (14 fl oz) **full-fat milk**
50 g (2 oz) **mature Cheddar
cheese**, grated
3 tablespoons chopped
parsley
1 **leek**, thinly sliced
1 **bay leaf**
500 g (1 lb) **mixed skinless
fish**, such as salmon, cod
and smoked haddock, diced
salt and **pepper**

Topping
20 g (¾ oz) **fresh
breadcrumbs**
40 g (1½ oz) **mature Cheddar
cheese**, grated

Preheat the slow cooker if necessary; see the manufacturer's instructions. Place the cornflour in a saucepan with a little of the milk and mix to a smooth paste. Stir in the remaining milk, then add the cheese, parsley, leek and bay leaf. Season to taste and bring to the boil, stirring. Cook until thickened.

Place the fish in the slow cooker pot. Pour over the hot leek sauce, cover and cook on low for 2–3 hours until the fish is cooked through.

Transfer the fish mixture to a shallow ovenproof dish, sprinkle the breadcrumbs and cheese over the top, then place under a preheated hot grill for 4–5 minutes until golden brown. Serve with steamed peas and mangetout, if liked.

For fish pies, follow the recipe above, omitting the breadcrumb and cheese topping. Peel and cut 625 g (1¼ lb) potatoes into chunks. Cook the potatoes in a saucepan of lightly salted boiling water for 15 minutes or until tender. Drain and mash with 4 tablespoons skimmed milk, then season and stir in 40 g (1½ oz) grated mature Cheddar cheese. Divide the cooked fish mixture between 4 individual pie dishes, spoon over the mash, rough up the top with a fork, then brush with 1 beaten egg. Cook under a preheated medium grill until golden.

chicken ramen

Preparation time **20 minutes**
Cooking temperature **low**
and **high**
Cooking time **6¼–8½ hours**
Serves **4**

1.25 litres (2¼ pints) **boiling
chicken stock**
3 tablespoons **soy sauce**,
plus extra to serve
2 teaspoons **fish sauce**
2 teaspoons **caster sugar**
½–1 teaspoon **crushed dried
red chillies** (to taste)
2–3 **garlic cloves**, finely
chopped
5 cm (2 inch) piece of **fresh
root ginger**, thinly sliced
4 **spring onions**, sliced
2 **star anise**
2 **dried kaffir lime leaves**
(optional)
625 g (1¼ lb) **boneless,
skinless chicken thighs**,
diced
125 g (4 oz) **instant plain** or
chicken ramen noodles
(discard the flavouring sachet
if using chicken noodles)
300 g (10 oz) **edamame bean
stir-fry mix**
handful of **coriander leaves**

Preheat the slow cooker if necessary; see the
manufacturer's instructions. Mix the boiling chicken
stock with the soy sauce, fish sauce and sugar, then
mix in the chillies to taste, the garlic, ginger, spring
onions, star anise and kaffir lime leaves, if using.

Put the diced chicken into the slow cooker pot and
pour over the boiling stock mixture. Cover with the
lid and cook on low for 6–8 hours until the chicken
is cooked through.

Increase the heat to high, then stir in the noodles and
stir-fry vegetables. Cook for 15–30 minutes until the
noodles are hot and the vegetables are just beginning
to soften.

Stir in the coriander, then ladle into deep bowls and
serve with extra soy sauce.

For salmon ramen, omit the chicken stock and
chicken and replace with fish or 1.25 litres (2 pints)
boiling vegetable stock and 4 x 125 g (4 oz) salmon
pieces. Cook on low for 1½– 2 hours until the salmon
is cooked through. Lift the salmon out, break it into
flakes and return it to the pot with the noodles and
edamame bean stir-fry mix. Continue as above.

red thai chicken curry

Preparation time **20 minutes**
Cooking temperature **low**
Cooking time **8¼–9½ hours**
Serves **4**

1 tablespoon **sunflower oil**
1 **onion**, finely chopped
2 tablespoons **red Thai curry paste**
2 teaspoons **galangal paste**
400 ml (14 fl oz) can **full-fat coconut milk**
200 ml (7 fl oz) **chicken stock**
2 teaspoons **fish sauce**
2 teaspoons **light muscovado sugar**
2 **dried kaffir lime leaves**
625 g (1¼ lb) **boneless, skinless chicken thighs**, cut into chunks
125 g (4 oz) **baby corn cobs**, thickly sliced
300 g (10 oz) **asparagus**, each spear trimmed and cut into 3 slices
75 g (3 oz) **mangetout**, halved
1 **carrot**, cut into matchsticks
coriander leaves, roughly chopped, to garnish

Preheat the slow cooker if necessary; see the manufacturer's instructions. Heat the sunflower oil in a saucepan, add the onion and fry it over a medium heat for 2–3 minutes. Stir in the curry paste and galangal, then mix in the coconut milk, stock, fish sauce, sugar and lime leaves and bring to the boil, stirring.

Add the chicken to the slow cooker pot, pour over the coconut milk mixture and make sure the chicken is below the liquid. Cover with the lid and cook on low for 8–9 hours until the chicken is cooked through.

Stir the curry, then add the vegetables and cook for 15–30 minutes until the vegetables are hot but still have a little bite.

Ladle into rice-lined bowls, if liked, and garnish with roughly chopped coriander leaves.

For red Thai beef curry, omit the chicken and add 625 g (1¼ lb) trimmed and cubed braising beef. Cook and serve as above.

duck confit

Preparation time **40 minutes**, plus salting **4 hours or overnight**
Cooking temperature **high**
Cooking time **3½–4 hours**
Serves **4**

4 **duck legs**, about 200 g (7 oz) each
3 tablespoons **coarse sea salt**
300 g (10 oz) jar **duck fat**, plus extra if needed
4 **garlic cloves**, sliced
2 **rosemary sprigs**
2 **thyme sprigs**
coarsely crushed **black pepper**

Place the duck in a single layer in a shallow dish and sprinkle with the salt. Chill for 4 hours or overnight.

Brush the salt from the duck and discard any juices in the dish. Preheat the slow cooker if necessary; see the manufacturer's instructions. Spoon the duck fat into the base of the slow cooker pot, add the garlic, herbs and pepper, then press the duck pieces down into the fat so that they fit together snugly in a single layer.

Cover with the lid and cook on high for 3½–4 hours or until the duck is cooked and beginning to fall off the bone.

Lift the duck out of the slow cooker and pack it into a large le parfait-style, wide-necked jar, pressing it down to minimize any air pockets. Strain the fat into the jar so that the top duck piece is well covered and any air pockets between the pieces of meat are filled with fat. If there isn't quite enough, top up with a little extra melted duck fat.

Cover with a lid and leave to cool, then transfer to the refrigerator and store for up to 1 week. When ready to serve, remove the duck pieces from the fat, scraping off most of the fat. Roast in a preheated oven, 220°C (425°F) Gas Mark 7, for 20 minutes until crisp and piping hot. Serve with a watercress, endive and orange salad, if liked, and duck-fat roasted potatoes (see below).

For duck-fat roasted potatoes, to serve as an accompaniment, cut 750 g (1½ lb) peeled potatoes into 2 cm (¾ inch) chunks, parboil for 4–5 minutes, then drain well. Melt 4 tablespoons of the duck fat in a roasting tin for 4–5 minutes, add the potatoes and toss in the fat. Roast in a preheated oven, 220°C (425°F) Gas Mark 7, for 30–35 minutes, turning once until golden.

madeira-braised pheasant

Preparation time **25 minutes**
Cooking temperature **low**
Cooking time **7–8 hours**
Serves **4**

2 **hen pheasants** or 1 **hen**
   and 1 **small cock pheasant**
   (ensure they will fit in the
   slow cooker pot)
25 g (1 oz) **butter**
1 tablespoon **olive oil**
2 **onions**, cut into wedges
125 g (4 oz) **smoked streaky
   bacon**, diced
125 ml (4 fl oz) **Madeira** or
   extra chicken stock,
   if preferred
300 ml (½ pint) **chicken stock**
1 tablespoon **redcurrant jelly**
175 g (6 oz) **cup mushrooms**,
   sliced
3 **thyme sprigs**
salt and **pepper**

Preheat the slow cooker if necessary; see the manufacturer's instructions. Season inside the body cavity of each pheasant with salt and pepper.

Heat the butter and oil in a large frying pan, add the pheasants, breast-side down, and fry over a medium heat until they are golden. Lift them out of the pan and put them on a plate.

Add the onion wedges and bacon to the pan and fry for 4–5 minutes, stirring, until golden. Pour in the Madeira, if using stock and redcurrant jelly and bring to the boil, stirring, until the jelly has melted. Season with salt and pepper.

Add the pheasants to the slow cooker pot breast-side down. If they are very snug, you may need to put them into the pot sideways. Add the mushrooms and thyme sprigs, then pour over the hot onion mixture.

Cover with the lid and cook on low for 7–8 hours or until the meat is beginning to come away from the bones and the juices run clear when the birds are pierced through the thickest part with a skewer or small knife.

Lift the birds out of the slow cooker pot and place them on a large plate. Scoop out the onions, bacon and mushrooms with a slotted spoon, place in a bowl, cover with foil and keep hot. Strain the stock mixture into a large frying pan and boil for 5–10 minutes until reduced and thickened.

Carve the breast meat and arrange it in shallow bowls. Spoon over the onion, bacon and mushrooms and serve with the sauce and mashed potatoes and green cabbage, if liked.

jerk pork with pineapple salsa

Preparation time **20 minutes**
Cooking temperature **high**
Cooking time **5–6 hours**
Serves **4**

750–900 g (1½–1¾ lb) **pork
  shoulder joint**
2 tablespoons **powdered jerk
  spice mix**
4 teaspoons **light muscovado
  sugar**
1 **onion**, roughly chopped
1 **carrot**, sliced
200 ml (7 fl oz) **boiling
  chicken stock**
salt and **pepper**

Pineapple salsa
1 small **pineapple**, trimmed
  and peeled
2 teaspoons **light muscovado
  sugar**
1 large **red chilli**, halved,
  deseeded and finely
  chopped
grated rind of 1 **lime**

Preheat the slow cooker if necessary; see the manufacturer's directions. Remove the string from the pork, then cut away the skin. Unroll and, if needed, make a slit in the meat so that it can be opened out to make a strip that is of an even thickness.

Rub the pork all over with the jerk spice mix, sugar and salt and pepper. Put the pork in the slow cooker pot, then scatter the onion and carrot into the gaps around the pork. Pour the boiling stock around the pork. Cover with the lid and cook on high for 5–6 hours until the meat is very tender and almost falls apart.

Meanwhile, slice the pineapple, cut away the core, then finely chop. Put it into a bowl with the sugar, chilli and lime rind. Mix together, then cover and chill until the pork is ready.

Lift the pork out of the slow cooker pot, remove any fat, then shred the meat with 2 forks. Serve with the salsa and rice mixed with canned black-eye peas, if liked.

For harissa pork with minted couscous, spread the pork with 4 teaspoons harissa, sugar and salt and pepper, add onion, carrot and stock and cook as above. Serve with 200 g (7 oz) couscous soaked in 400 ml (14 fl oz) boiling water for 5 minutes, then mix with the grated rind and juice of 1 lemon, 2 tablespoons olive oil and a handful of chopped mint and 3 finely chopped spring onions.

lettuce wrappers

Preparation time **20 minutes**
Cooking temperature **low**
Cooking time **8–9 hours**
Serves **4**

1 tablespoon **sunflower oil**
750 g (1½ lb) **stewing beef**,
  cut into small cubes
1 **onion**, chopped
2 **garlic cloves**, finely chopped
2 tablespoons **plain flour**
350 ml (12 fl oz) **beef stock**
1 teaspoon **crushed dried
  red chillies**
½ teaspoon **chilli powder**
2 tablespoons **soy sauce**
2 tablespoons **hoisin sauce**
2 tablespoons **rice vinegar**
1 tablespoon **dark
  muscovado sugar**
salt and **pepper**

To serve
1 **iceberg lettuce**
1 small **red onion**, thinly sliced
small handful of **coriander**,
  roughly chopped

Preheat the slow cooker if necessary; see the manufacturer's instructions. Heat the oil in a large frying pan, add the beef a few pieces at a time, then fry over a high heat, stirring, until browned.

Add the onion and garlic and fry for 3–4 minutes until softened. Sprinkle over the flour and mix it in, then gradually mix in the stock. Sprinkle over the chillies and chilli powder, then stir in the soy and hoisin sauces, vinegar and sugar. Season with a little pepper.

Bring to the boil, then transfer to the slow cooker pot. Press the meat beneath the liquid, cover with the lid and cook on low for 8–9 hours until the beef is tender.

Separate the lettuce leaves, spoon a little of the beef into each lettuce cup, then sprinkle with the red onion and coriander. To eat, you fold the leaves over the beef filling to pick up the parcels or eat them with a knife and fork.

For beef 'Peking duck' wrappers, make and cook the beef as above. Warm 16 Chinese pancakes in a steamer according to the packet instructions. Separate the pancakes, top with spoonfuls of the hot beef, ½ cucumber cut into matchstick strips and 1 bunch of spring onions, cut into matchstick strips. Roll up and serve immediately.

sunday best beef

Preparation time **20 minutes**
Cooking temperature **low**
Cooking time **8–9 hours**
Serves **4**

2 tablespoons **plain flour**
750 g (1½ lb) piece of **blade braising beef**, cut into 2 cm (¾ inch) thick slices
2 tablespoons **olive oil**
300 g (10 oz) **shallots**, peeled
150 ml (¼ pint) **red wine** or **extra beef stock**, if preferred
300 ml (½ pint) **beef stock**
1 tablespoon **tomato purée**
1 teaspoon **dried mixed herbs**
1 teaspoon **Dijon mustard**
125 g (4 oz) **cup mushrooms**, sliced
salt and **pepper**

To serve
4 large **ready-made Yorkshire puddings**
new potatoes
selection of vegetables

Preheat the slow cooker if necessary; see the manufacturer's instructions. Mix the flour and a little salt and pepper together on a plate, then coat both sides of the beef slices with the seasoned flour.

Heat 1 tablespoon of the oil in a large frying pan, add the beef slices and fry until browned on both sides. Lift out the beef and transfer it to the slow cooker pot. Add the remaining oil and fry the shallots for a few minutes until they are just beginning to brown.

Sprinkle over any remaining seasoned flour, then mix in the wine, if using, stock, tomato purée, herbs and mustard. Bring to the boil, stirring.

Add the mushrooms to the slow cooker pot, then pour over the shallot mix. Press the beef below the surface of the liquid, cover with the lid and cook on low for 8–9 hours or until the beef is tender.

When almost ready to serve, heat the Yorkshire puddings in the oven according to the packet instructions. Steam the vegetables, then transfer the Yorkshire puddings to serving plates and fill with the beef, sauce and steamed veggies.

For poor man's Sunday best, grill 8 large pork sausages until browned but not cooked through. Add to the slow cooker pot. Fry the shallots in a little oil, sprinkle with the flour, then add 150 g (5 oz) passata instead of the wine, mix in the remaining ingredients and cook and serve as above.

lamb & mushroom suet pudding

Preparation time **35 minutes**
Cooking temperature **high**
Cooking time **5–6 hours**
Serves **4**

25 g (1 oz) **butter**, plus extra
for greasing
1 tablespoon **olive oil**
1 **onion**, thinly sliced
150 g (5 oz) **cup mushrooms**,
sliced
500 g (1 lb) **lamb fillet**, diced
1 tablespoon **Worcestershire
sauce**
5 tablespoons **ruby port** or
red wine or **extra lamb
stock**, if preferred
5 tablespoons **lamb stock**
leaves from **2 rosemary
sprigs**, chopped
salt and **pepper**

Suet pastry
300 g (10 oz) **self-raising
flour**
150 g (5 oz) **vegetable suet**
leaves from 3 **rosemary
sprigs**, chopped
200 ml (7 fl oz) **cold water**

Preheat the slow cooker if necessary; see the
manufacturer's instructions. Grease a 1.25 litre (2¼ pint)
pudding basin. Heat the butter and oil in a frying pan, add
the onion and fry for 5 minutes until golden. Add the
mushrooms and lamb and fry for 5 minutes, stirring, until
browned. Add the Worcestershire sauce, port or wine,
if using, stock and rosemary. Season and set aside.

Make the pastry. Place the flour, suet and rosemary
in a large bowl, season generously and stir together.
Gradually mix in the cold water to make a soft but not
sticky dough, adding extra if needed. Lightly knead the
dough, then roll it out thickly on a lightly floured surface
to make a rough circle about 33 cm (13 inches) in
diameter. Cut a one-quarter wedge out of the circle and
reserve this for the lid. Lift the remaining piece into the
pudding basin, butting the cut edges together, then press
together to seal and press the pastry over the basin.

Spoon in the lamb mixture. Pat and roll the reserved
pastry into a circle the same size as the top of the basin,
stick it in place with a little water, then trim off any excess
pastry. Cover with a dome of buttered foil, then stand the
basin in the slow cooker pot. Pour boiling water into the
slow cooker pot so that it reaches halfway up the sides
of the basin. Cover with the lid and cook on high for
5–6 hours until the pastry is light and fluffy and the lamb
is tender. Lift the basin out of the slow cooker with oven
gloves. Serve with mashed swede and carrots, if liked.

For steak & mushroom pudding, replace the lamb with
500 g (1 lb) sliced rump steak and add 150 ml (¼ pint)
brown ale or extra stock and 2 teaspoons light muscovado
sugar in place of the port and thyme. Make as above.

rioja-braised lamb with olives

Preparation time **20 minutes**
Cooking temperature **high**
Cooking time **5–6 hours**
Serves **4**

2 tablespoons **olive oil**
4 **lamb shanks**, 1.5 kg (3 lb)
  in total
2 **red onions**, cut into wedges
4 large **garlic cloves**, halved
300 ml (½ pint) **Rioja red
  wine** or **lamb stock**
400 g (13 oz) can **chopped
  tomatoes**
1 tablespoon **redcurrant jelly**
3 **rosemary sprigs**
150 g (5 oz) **mixed pitted
  olives**
salt and **pepper**

Preheat the slow cooker if necessary; see the
manufacturer's instructions. Heat 1 tablespoon of the
oil in a large frying pan, season the lamb shanks, then
add them to the pan and brown on all sides. Lift them
out of the pan and put them in the slow cooker pot
with the meatiest parts downwards.

Add the remaining oil and onion wedges to the pan
and fry for 3–4 minutes until just beginning to colour.
Add the garlic, wine or stock, tomatoes, redcurrant jelly
and rosemary. Season with salt and pepper and bring
to the boil, stirring.

Scatter the olives over the lamb, then pour over the
hot onion mixture. Cover with the lid and cook on high
for 5–6 hours until the lamb is very tender.

When ready to serve, pour the liquid out of the
slow cooker into a saucepan and boil for 10 minutes
until reduced by half. Put the lamb into shallow bowls
lined with some runny polenta flavoured with butter
and Parmesan or mashed potato, if liked, spoon over
the onions and olives, then serve with the Rioja sauce.

For Rioja-braised chicken with olives, substitute a
1.5 kg (3 lb) chicken for the lamb shanks and cook as
above, with the chicken cooked breast-side down in
the liquid, until the chicken is cooked through.

peppered venison with scones

Preparation time **35 minutes**
Cooking temperature **low**
and **high**
Cooking time **8¾—11 hours**
Serves **4**

25 g (1 oz) **butter**
1 tablespoon **olive oil**
750 g (1½ lb) **venison
shoulder**, diced
1 large **red onion**, sliced
125 g (4 oz) **cup mushrooms**,
sliced
2 **garlic cloves**, chopped
2 tablespoons **plain flour**
200 ml (7 fl oz) **red wine** or
extra chicken stock
250 ml (8 fl oz) **chicken stock**
2 teaspoons **tomato purée**
2 tablespoons **redcurrant jelly**
1 teaspoon crushed **peppercorns**
salt

Scones

250 g (8 oz) **self-raising flour**
40 g (1½ oz) **butter**, diced
125 g (4 oz) **Gorgonzola
cheese**, finely crumbled
3 tablespoons chopped
parsley or **chives**
1 **egg**, beaten
4–5 tablespoons **milk**

Preheat the slow cooker if necessary; see the manufacturer's instructions. Heat the butter and oil in a large frying pan, add the diced venison a few pieces at time, then fry until evenly browned. Transfer to a plate.

Add the onion to the pan and fry for 5 minutes. Stir in the mushrooms, garlic and flour and cook for 1 minute. Stir in the wine, if using, stock, tomato purée, redcurrant jelly, peppercorns and salt and bring to the boil.

Arrange the venison in the slow cooker pot, add the hot stock mixture and press the venison below the surface. Cover with the lid and cook on low for 8–10 hours until the venison is tender.

When the venison is tender, make the scones. Put the flour in a bowl, add the butter and rub it into the flour with your fingertips until the mixture resembles fine breadcrumbs. Stir in a little salt and pepper, the cheese and herbs. Reserve 1 tablespoon of egg for glazing and add the rest. Gradually mix in enough milk to make a soft dough.

Knead lightly, then pat the dough into a thick oval or a round that is a little smaller than the top of your slow cooker. Cut it into 8 wedges and arrange these, spaced slightly apart, on top of the venison. Cover and cook on high for 45 minutes—1 hour until the dough topping has turned golden.

Lift the pot out of the machine using oven gloves, brush the scones with the reserved egg and brown under a preheated hot grill. Serve with green beans, if liked.

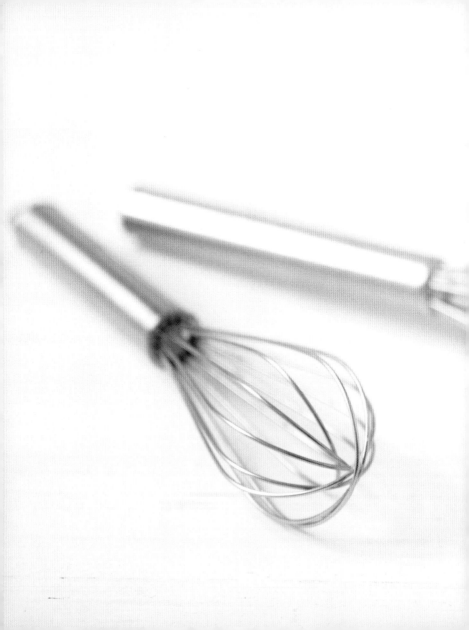

nostalgic puds

apple & pecan cake

Preparation time **30 minutes**,
  plus cooling
Cooking temperature **high**
Cooking time **3½–4 hours**
Serves **6**

100 g (3½ oz) **butter**, plus
  extra for greasing
100 g (3½ oz) **light
  muscovado sugar**
75 g (3 oz) **golden syrup**
175 g (6 oz) **self-raising flour**
1 teaspoon **bicarbonate
  of soda**
1 teaspoon **ground cinnamon**
1 teaspoon **ground ginger**
2 **eggs**, beaten
1 **dessert apple**, cored and
  grated (no need to peel)
40 g (1½ oz) **pecan nuts**,
  broken into pieces, plus extra
  to serve
280 g (9 oz) **cream cheese**
50 g (2 oz) **icing sugar**, sifted,
  plus extra to decorate
½ teaspoon **orange extract**

Preheat the slow cooker if necessary; see the
manufacturer's instructions. Butter the inside of a 15 cm
(6 inch) diameter soufflé dish that is 8 cm (3¼ inches)
high. Line the base with a circle of nonstick baking paper.

Heat the butter, sugar and syrup together in a saucepan
over a gentle heat. Take the pan off the heat to cool slightly.

Mix the flour, bicarbonate of soda and ground spices
together, then stir into the butter mixture with the
beaten eggs and grated apple. Mix until smooth, then
mix in the pecan nuts.

Pour into the buttered dish, cover with a dome of
buttered foil and stand in the slow cooker pot. Pour
boiling water into the cooker pot around the dish so that
it reaches halfway up the sides of the dish. Cover with
the lid and cook on high for 3½–4 hours or until well
risen and a skewer comes out clean when inserted
into the cake.

Lift out the soufflé dish with oven gloves, remove the
foil and leave to cool for 15 minutes. Loosen the edge
of the cake, turn out on to a wire rack and peel off the
lining paper. Leave to cool completely.

When ready to serve, beat the cream cheese, icing
sugar and orange extract together. Transfer the cake to
a serving plate, spread the icing over the top and sides
of the cake and sprinkle with extra pecan nut pieces
and dust. Serve with a sifted icing sugar.

For carrot & walnut cake, omit the apple and pecan
nuts and add 125 g (4 oz) grated carrot and 40 g
(1½ oz) chopped walnuts. Cook as above.

strawberry cheesecake

Preparation time **30 minutes**,
  plus chilling
Cooking temperature **high**
Cooking time **2–2½ hours**
Serves **4–5**

4 **trife sponges**
300 g (10 oz) **full-fat cream
  cheese**
75 g (3 oz) **caster sugar**
150 ml (¼ pint) **double cream**
3 **eggs**
grated rind and juice of
  ½ **lemon**

Topping
2 tablespoons **strawberry jam**
1 tablespoon **lemon juice**
200 g (7 oz) **strawberries**,
  hulled and sliced

Preheat the slow cooker if necessary; see the manufacturer's instructions. Line the base and sides of a soufflé dish, 14 cm (5½ inches) in diameter and 9 cm (3½ inches) high, with nonstick baking paper, checking first that it will fit in the slow cooker pot. Line the base with the trifle sponges, trimming to fit in a single layer.

Put the cream cheese and sugar in a bowl, then gradually whisk in the cream until smooth and thick. Gradually whisk in the eggs 1 at a time, then mix in the lemon rind and juice. Pour the mixture into the dish and spread it to level out the surface.

Cover the top with buttered foil and lower it into the slow cooker pot. Pour boiling water into the pot to come halfway up the sides of the dish. Cover with the lid and cook on high for 2–2½ hours or until the cheesecake is well risen and softly set in the centre.

Lift the dish out of the slow cooker pot using oven gloves and leave the cheesecake to cool and firm up. It will sink quickly as it cools. Transfer to the refrigerator to chill for at least 4 hours.

Loosen the edge of the cheesecake with a knife, turn out on to a serving plate, peel off the lining paper and turn it the right way up. Mix the jam and lemon juice in a bowl until smooth, add the sliced strawberries and toss together. Spoon the strawberry mixture on top of the cheesecake and serve immediately.

For blueberry cheesecake, mix 2 tablespoons blueberry jam with 1 tablespoon orange juice and 150 g (5 oz) blueberries. Spoon over the cooled cheesecake and serve immediately.

christmas pudding

Preparation time **20 minutes**
Cooking temperature **high**
Cooking time **7–8 hours**
Reheating time **2–2½ hours**
Serves **6–8**

butter, for greasing
750 g (1½ lb) **mixed luxury dried fruit** (with larger fruits diced)
50 g (2 oz) **pistachio nuts**, roughly chopped
25 g (1 oz) **glacé** or **stem ginger**, finely chopped
1 **dessert apple**, peeled, cored and coarsely grated
grated rind and juice of
   1 lemon
grated rind and juice of
   1 orange
4 tablespoons **brandy**, plus another 4 tablespoons to serve (optional)
50 g (2 oz) **soft dark muscovado sugar**
50 g (2 oz) **self-raising flour**
75 g (3 oz) **breadcrumbs**
100 g (3½ oz) **vegetable suet**
1 teaspoon **ground mixed spice**
2 **eggs**, beaten

Preheat the slow cooker if necessary; see the manufacturer's instructions. Check that a 1.5 litre (2½ pint) pudding basin will fit inside your slow cooker pot with a little room to spare, then butter the inside of the basin and line the base with a circle of nonstick baking paper.

Put the dried fruit, nuts, ginger and grated apple into a large bowl. Add the citrus rinds and juice and brandy and mix together well. Stir in the remaining ingredients. Spoon into the buttered basin, pressing down well as you go. Cover with a large circle of nonstick baking paper, then a piece of foil. Tie the foil to the basin with string and add a string handle. Lower the basin into the slow cooker pot using foil straps (see page 15) and pour boiling water into the pot to come two-thirds of the way up the sides of the basin. Cover with the lid and cook on high for 7–8 hours. Check halfway through cooking and top up with extra boiling water if needed. Take out of the slow cooker and leave to cool.

Cover with fresh foil, leaving the baking paper in place. Retie with string and keep in a cool place for 2 months or until Christmas.

When ready to serve, preheat the slow cooker if needed, add the pudding and boiling water as above and reheat on high for 2—2½ hours. Remove the foil and paper, loosen the pudding and turn out. Warm the brandy in a saucepan, if using. When it is just boiling, flame with a taper and quickly pour over the pudding. Serve with brandy butter or cream, if liked.

chocolate & guinness sponge

Preparation time **35 minutes**,
  plus cooling
Cooking temperature **high**
Cooking time **2–2½ hours**
Serves **6**

75 g (3 oz) **butter**, softened,
  plus extra for greasing
40 g (1½ oz) **cocoa powder**,
  plus extra for dusting
175 g (6 oz) **plain flour**
1 teaspoon **bicarbonate of soda**
½ teaspoon **baking powder**
175 g (6 oz) **light muscovado
  sugar**
2 **eggs**
200 ml (7 fl oz) **Guinness**

Sauce
125 ml (4 fl oz) **Guinness**
50 g (2 oz) **light muscovado
  sugar**
100 g (3½ oz) **plain dark
  chocolate**, broken into pieces
1 teaspoon **cornflour** mixed to
  a paste with a little water

Topping
2 tablespoons **light
  muscovado sugar**
300 ml (½ pint) **double cream**
75 g (3 oz) **white chocolate**

Preheat the slow cooker if necessary; see the
manufacturer's instructions. Grease a 15 cm (6 inch)
diameter round ovenproof dish that is 8 cm (3¼ inches)
deep. Line the base with nonstick baking paper.

Sift the cocoa powder, flour, bicarbonate of soda and
baking powder into a bowl and stir together. Cream the
butter and sugar together in a separate large bowl or
using a food processor. Beat in the eggs 1 at a time
until smooth, then add the cocoa mix and gradually
beat in the Guinness until smooth.

Spoon the mixture into the prepared dish. Cover with
a dome of buttered foil and put it into the slow cooker
pot. Pour boiling water around the pudding dish so that it
reaches halfway up the sides of the dish. Cover and cook
on high for 2–2½ hours until the pudding is well risen
and a skewer inserted into the centre comes out clean.

Lift the pudding dish out of the slow cooker pot with
oven gloves and leave to stand for 20 minutes. Loosen
the cake edge and turn out the cake on to a wire rack.
Peel away the lining paper and leave to cool completely.

Put all the sauce ingredients into a small saucepan and
heat gently until the chocolate has melted, then bring just
to the boil, stirring, until thickened. Take the pan off the
heat, cover and leave the sauce to cool. For the topping,
stir the sugar into the cream and chill in the refrigerator.
Cut the cake in half horizontally, whisk the cream until it
forms soft swirls, then spread over the cakes and arrange
the cakes separately on a large board. Coarsely grate the
white chocolate on top and dust with sifted cocoa. Cut
into wedges and serve drizzled with the warmed sauce.

peach & raspberry cobbler

Preparation time **25 minutes**
Cooking temperature **high**
Cooking time **2½–3¼ hours**
Serves **6**

6 **peaches,** about 750 g
  (1½ lb) in total, halved,
  stoned
  and cut into chunks
50 g (2 oz) **caster sugar**
juice of 1 **lemon**
250 g (8 oz) **raspberries**

Topping
125 g (4 oz) **self-raising flour**
50 g (2 oz) **caster sugar**
grated rind of 1 **lemon**
50 g (2 oz) **butter,** cubed
1 **egg,** beaten
4 tablespoons **semi-skimmed milk**
little **icing sugar,** sifted,
  to decorate

Preheat the slow cooker if necessary; see the manufacturer's instructions. Add the peaches, sugar and lemon juice to the slow cooker pot. Cover and cook on high for 1½–2 hours or until the peaches have softened.

Make the topping. Put the flour, sugar, lemon rind and butter in a bowl and rub the butter into the flour with your fingertips or an electric mixer until the mixture resembles fine breadcrumbs. Stir in half the egg (reserve the rest for glazing) and enough milk to blend to a soft, spoonable mixture.

Stir the peaches, then sprinkle over the raspberries. Spoon the cobbler topping in blobs over the fruit. Cover with the lid and cook on high for 1–1¼ hours until the topping is set and risen.

Take the pot out of the machine with oven gloves, brush the top with the remaining egg, then brown under a preheated hot grill. Decorate with a little sifted icing sugar and serve hot with cream or vanilla ice cream, if liked.

For apple & berry cobbler, put 750 g (1½ lb) cooking apples, peeled, cored and cut into chunks, in a slow cooker pot with 75 g (3 oz) sugar and lemon juice. Cook as above, then stir in 125 g (4 oz) raspberries and 125 g (4 oz) blackberries and add the cobbler topping. Continue as above.

plum & blueberry betty

Preparation time **20 minutes**
Cooking temperature **high**
Cooking time **2½–3 hours**
Serves **6**

500 g (1 lb) **red plums**,
 halved, pitted and sliced
150 g (5 oz) **blueberries**
75 g (3 oz) **caster sugar**
juice of **1 orange**
3 tablespoons **water**

Topping
75 g (3 oz) **butter**
100 g (3½ oz) **white bread**,
 torn into small pieces
50 g (2 oz) **demerara sugar**
40 g (1½ oz) **flaked almonds**
large pinch of **ground
 cinnamon**

Preheat the slow cooker if necessary; see the manufacturer's instructions. Add the plums and blueberries to the slow cooker pot, sprinkle over the sugar, then add the orange juice and measurement water. Cover with the lid and cook on high for 2½–3 hours until the fruit is soft.

When almost ready to serve, heat the butter in a frying pan, add the bread, sugar and almonds, sprinkle with a little cinnamon and fry over a medium heat, stirring, until the bread and almonds are crisp and golden.

Ladle the fruit into bowls, sprinkle the topping over and serve with scoops of vanilla ice cream, if liked.

For mixed berry Betty, add 400 g (13 oz) hulled and halved strawberries to the slow cooker pot with 200 g (7 oz) raspberries and 150 g (5 oz) blueberries, then add the sugar and orange juice, omitting the water. Cook and serve as above.

sticky toffee pudding

Preparation time **25 minutes**, plus standing
Cooking temperature **high**
Cooking time **2½–3 hours**
Serves **6**

125 g (4 oz) **pitted dates**, chopped
1 teaspoon **bicarbonate of soda**
250 ml (8 fl oz) **boiling water**
50 g (2 oz) **butter**, at room temperature, plus extra for greasing
175 g (6 oz) **plain flour**
1 teaspoon **baking powder**
125 g (4 oz) **light muscovado sugar**
1 **egg**
1 teaspoon **vanilla extract**

Toffee sauce
75 g (3 oz) **butter**
125 g (4 oz) **light muscovado sugar**
150 ml (¼ pint) **double cream**

Put the dates and bicarbonate of soda in a small bowl, pour over the boiling water and stir together, then leave to stand for 30 minutes. Grease a 15 cm (6 inch) diameter soufflé dish or 1.2 litre (2 pint) round ovenproof dish with a little butter.

Preheat the slow cooker if necessary; see the manufacturer's instructions. Mix the plain flour and baking powder together in a bowl. Cream the butter and sugar in a large bowl or food processor, then beat in the egg and vanilla until smooth. Add the flour and soaked dates, with any soaking liquid, and beat well.

Spoon the mixture into the buttered dish, level off the surface, then cover with a domed piece of buttered foil. Place the dish in the slow cooker pot, then pour boiling water around the pudding dish so that it reaches halfway up the sides of the dish. Cover with the lid and cook on high for 2½–3 hours or until the pudding is deep brown, well risen, the top is dry and a skewer comes out clean when inserted into the centre. Take the pudding out of the slow cooker with oven gloves.

Put all the sauce ingredients in a medium saucepan and heat gently, stirring, until the sugar has dissolved and the butter has melted. Increase the heat slightly and cook for 2–3 minutes, stirring constantly, until the sauce has thickened slightly and smells of toffee. Cool a little. Spoon the pudding into bowls, drizzle over the hot sauce and serve with scoops of vanilla ice cream, if liked.

For sticky chocolate toffee pudding, sift 150 g (5 oz) plain flour and 25 g (1 oz) cocoa powder together and mix with the baking powder, then make as above.

pineapple & rum upside-down pud

Preparation time **20 minutes**
Cooking temperature **high**
Cooking time **4–4½ hours**
Serves **6**

butter, for greasing
3 tablespoons **light muscovado sugar**
2 x 220 g (7½ oz) cans **pineapple rings**, drained
about 6 **glacé cherries**
3 tablespoons **golden syrup**
2 tablespoons **dark rum**

Sponge
100 g (3½ oz) **soft margarine**
100 g (3½ oz) **light muscovado sugar**
175 g (6 oz) **self-raising flour**
2 teaspoons **ground ginger**
2 **eggs**
1 tablespoon **dark rum**

Preheat the slow cooker if necessary; see the manufacturer's instructions. Lightly butter a 1.5 litre (2½ pint) pudding basin. Line the base with a circle of nonstick baking paper and grease this circle, too. Sprinkle the sugar over the base and sides.

Arrange the drained pineapple slices in the basin, over the base and around the sides, then add a cherry to the centre of each slice. Finely chop the remaining pineapple and set aside. Add the golden syrup and rum to the base of the basin.

Make the sponge. Put all the ingredients into a mixing bowl and beat with an electric mixer until smooth. Stir in the chopped pineapple, then spoon the mixture into the pineapple-lined basin. Spread out the mixture to level off the surface. Cover the basin with a dome of buttered foil, then stand the basin in the slow cooker pot. Pour boiling water into the pot around the basin so that it reaches halfway up the sides of the basin. Cover and cook on high for 4–4½ hours or until the sponge is well risen, dry to the touch and a skewer comes out clean when inserted into the centre.

Lift the basin out of the slow cooker with oven gloves. Remove the foil, loosen the edge of the sponge, then turn out on to a plate. Peel off the base paper. Serve scoops of the sponge in bowls drizzled with hot custard, if liked.

For pineapple & orange upside-down pudding,
finely grate 1 large orange and squeeze the juice. Add 2 tablespoons of the juice to the pudding basin instead of the rum, then add the grated rind and 1 more tablespoon of the juice to the sponge. Cook as above.

190

marbled chocolate & banana pud

Preparation time **20 minutes**
Cooking temperature **high**
Cooking time **3–3½ hours**
Serves **6**

1 tablespoon **cocoa powder**
½ teaspoon **ground
  cinnamon**
4 teaspoons **boiling water**
125 g (4 oz) **soft margarine**
125 g (4 oz) **caster sugar**
125 g (4 oz) **self-raising flour**
2 **eggs**
½ teaspoon **vanilla extract**
1 small **banana** (about 125 g/
  4 oz when weighed with skin
  on), peeled and mashed
1 **Mars bar**, sliced, to decorate

Chocolate sauce
2 **Mars bars**, sliced
4 tablespoons **milk**

Preheat the slow cooker if necessary; see the manufacturer's instructions. Lightly grease a 500 g (1 lb) loaf tin (do check that it will fit into your slow cooker pot first and, if not, use a round ovenproof dish) and line the base with a piece of nonstick baking paper.

Mix the cocoa, cinnamon and boiling water together in a bowl until smooth, then leave to cool. Put the margarine into a bowl or food processor, add the sugar, flour, eggs and vanilla and beat together well. Spoon half the sponge mixture into a separate bowl, then beat in the cocoa mixture until smooth. Stir the banana into the sponge mix that is not flavoured with cocoa and cinnamon.

Add alternate spoonfuls of cocoa and banana mixture to the prepared loaf tin, then run a small knife through the mixtures to marble the batter colours. Cover the dish with a greased dome of foil, then put the tin into the slow cooker pot. Pour boiling water into the pot around the tin so that it reaches halfway up the sides. Cover with the lid and cook on high for 3–3½ hours or until the top of the sponge is dry, well risen and a skewer comes out clean when inserted into the centre. Take the tin out of the slow cooker using oven gloves.

Warm the Mars bars and milk in a saucepan, stirring, until smooth. Strain, if needed. Loosen the sides of the pudding and turn it out, then decorate with slices of Mars bar. Cut the pudding into thick slices and serve with the sauce and a scoop of vanilla ice cream, if liked.

For marbled chocolate & orange sponge pud, make the recipe as above, omitting the mashed banana and replacing it with the grated rind of 1 orange.

tutti-frutti spotted dick

Preparation time **20 minutes**
Cooking temperature **high**
Cooking time **2½–3½ hours**
Serves **6**

oil or **butter**, for greasing
3 tablespoons **apricot jam**
250 g (8 oz) **self-raising flour**
125 g (4 oz) **vegetable suet**
50 g (2 oz) **caster sugar**
grated rind of 1 **orange**
grated rind of 1 **lemon**
40 g (1½ oz) **dried
    cranberries**
65 g (2½ oz) **sultanas**
100 g (3½ oz) **ready-to-eat
    dried apricots**, diced
1 **egg**, beaten
200–250 ml (7–8 fl oz)
    semi-skimmed milk

Preheat the slow cooker if necessary; see the manufacturer's instructions. Grease a 1.2 litre (2 pint) pudding basin with a little oil or butter, then line the base with a circle of nonstick baking paper. Spoon the jam into the base of the prepared basin.

Put the flour, suet, sugar and grated citrus rinds in a mixing bowl, then add the dried fruits and stir together. Pour in the egg, then mix in enough milk to make it a soft, spoonable mixture. Spoon the mixture into the jam-lined basin and level off the surface. Cover with oiled or buttered foil in a slight dome shape so there is room for the pudding to rise.

Put the basin into the slow cooker pot, then pour enough boiling water into the pot around the basin for it to reach halfway up the sides of the basin. Cover with the lid and cook on high for 2½–3½ hours until the pudding is light and fluffy.

Lift the pudding basin out of the slow cooker pot with oven gloves and remove the foil. Loosen the edge of the pudding with a knife and turn it out on to a plate. Scoop it into bowls and serve with hot vanilla custard, if liked.

For coconut & apricot spotted Dick, mix the dry ingredients and citrus rinds together. Omit the dried cranberries and sultanas and add 40 g (1½ oz) desiccated coconut, 25 g (1 oz) finely chopped candied peel and 150 g (5 oz) diced ready-to-eat dried apricots instead. Continue as above.

mini blackberry suet puds

Preparation time **30 minutes**
Cooking temperature **high**
Cooking time **3½–4 hours**
Serves **4**

butter, for greasing
250 g (8 oz) **self-raising flour**,
  plus extra for dusting
125 g (4 oz) **vegetable suet**
100 g (3½ oz) **caster sugar**
grated rind of 1 **lemon**
150 ml (¼ pint) **cold water**
200 g (7 oz) **blackberries**
2 large **red plums**, halved,
  pitted and diced
few drops of **vanilla extract**

Preheat the slow cooker if necessary; see the manufacturer's instructions. Grease 4 x 250 ml (8 fl oz) metal pudding tins (check first that they will fit together in the slow cooker pot). Put the flour, suet, half the sugar and the grated lemon rind in a mixing bowl. Mix in enough of the water to create a soft but not sticky dough.

Divide the dough into 4 equal portions, then roll out the first piece on a lightly floured surface into a 15 cm (6 inch) circle. Cut out a one-quarter wedge and reserve this for the top. Lift the remaining dough circle into one of the pudding tins, press it gently in and allow it to stick out a little above the tin. Press the cut edges together to seal. Repeat with the remaining 3 portions of dough. Fill the tins with the fruit and the remaining sugar and vanilla.

Pat each remaining piece of dough into a circle, then roll it out until it is large enough to cover the top of a tin. Stick it in place with a little water, then trim off any excess. Pierce the centre of each lid, then cover each pud with a dome of buttered foil. Stand the pudding tins in the slow cooker pot and pour enough boiling water into the pot to reach halfway up the sides of the tins. Cover and cook on high for 3½–4 hours until the pastry is light and fluffy. Lift the puddings out of the slow cooker using oven gloves, then remove the foil and loosen the edges with a round-bladed knife. Turn out into shallow bowls and serve drizzled with hot custard, if liked.

For mini apricot suet puddings, make the pastry and line the tins as above. Fill with the remaining sugar and 375 g (12 oz) pitted and diced fresh apricots mixed with 1 tablespoon chopped stem ginger in syrup, adding 1 tablespoon of the ginger syrup. Continue as above.

blackberry & apple eton mess

Preparation time **20 minutes**,
  plus chilling
Cooking temperature **high**
Cooking time **2½–3½ hours**
Serves **6**

625 g (1¼ lb) **cooking apples**
  (about 2), peeled, cored
  and chopped
150 g (5 oz) **blackberries**
125 g (4 oz) **caster sugar**
3 tablespoons **water**

To serve
300 ml (½ pint) **double cream**
150 g (5 oz) **natural yogurt**
2 tablespoons **lemon curd**
3 **ready-made individual
  meringue nests**

Preheat the slow cooker if necessary; see the
manufacturer's instructions. Add the apple and
blackberries to the slow cooker pot, sprinkle over the
sugar, then add the measurement water. Cover with the
lid and cook on high for 2½–3½ hours until the fruit is
softened. Stir well, then remove the pot from the slow
cooker and leave to cool.

Whip the cream lightly about 30 minutes before
serving, then fold in the yogurt and lemon curd. Crumble
the meringues into pieces and fold about three-quarters
of the meringue pieces into the cream.

Spoon the fruit compote and cream mixture alternately
into 6 glasses, then run a teaspoon through them to
marble the mixtures together. Sprinkle the tops with
the remaining meringue pieces and chill for up to
30 minutes until ready to serve (any longer and the
meringue will begin to dissolve).

For peach & raspberry Eton mess, add 625 g
(1¼ lb) stoned and diced peaches to the slow cooker
pot with 50 g (2 oz) caster sugar and the juice of
1 lemon. Cover and cook on high for 1½ –2 hours until
softened. Stir in 250 g (8 oz) raspberries, re-cover and
cook for 15 minutes, then leave to cool. Layer with the
cream mixture and meringues as above.

baked honey & orange custards

Preparation time **15 minutes**, plus chilling
Cooking temperature **low**
Cooking time **4–5 hours**
Serves **4**

2 **eggs**
2 **egg yolks**
400 ml (14 fl oz) **semi-skimmed milk**
3 teaspoons **caster sugar**
3 teaspoons **clear honey**
½ teaspoon **vanilla extract**
finely grated rind of ½ **orange**
large pinch of **ground cinnamon**

Preheat the slow cooker if necessary; see the manufacturer's instructions. Place the eggs, egg yolks and milk in a mixing bowl with the sugar, honey and vanilla and whisk together until smooth. Strain the mixture through a sieve into a large jug, then whisk in the orange rind.

Divide the mixture equally between 4 x 150 ml (¼ pint) ovenproof dishes (checking first that they will fit in your slow cooker pot together). Place the dishes in the slow cooker pot and sprinkle the cinnamon over the top. Pour hot water into the slow cooker pot around the dishes until it reaches halfway up the sides of the dishes. Cover the tops of the dishes with domed foil, cover with the lid and cook on low for 4–5 hours until set.

Remove the dishes from the slow cooker and leave to cool. Transfer to the refrigerator to chill well for 3–4 hours before serving.

For vanilla crème brûlée, follow the recipe above to cook and chill the custards, using 1 teaspoon vanilla extract and omitting the orange rind and cinnamon. Just before serving, sprinkle 1 teaspoon caster sugar over the top of each dish and caramelize the sugar with a cook's blowtorch or under a preheated hot grill. Cool for a few minutes to allow the sugar to set hard, then serve with a few fresh raspberries.

chocolate crème caramels

Preparation time **25 minutes**,
  plus chilling
Cooking temperature **low**
Cooking time **3–4 hours**
Serves **4**

2 tablespoons **cocoa powder**
2 teaspoons **instant coffee**
2 tablespoons **boiling water**
2 **eggs**
2 **egg yolks**
2 tablespoons **caster sugar**
450 ml (¾ pint) **semi-
  skimmed milk**

Caramel
100 g (3½ oz) **granulated
  sugar**
6 tablespoons **cold water**
2 tablespoons **boiling water**

Preheat the slow cooker if necessary. For the caramel, place the sugar in a heavy-based saucepan with the cold water. Cook over a low heat, without stirring, until the sugar has completely dissolved. Increase the heat and boil for 5–8 minutes or until rich golden brown.

Remove the pan from the heat and add the boiling water, taking care as the syrup can spit. Keeping the pan at arm's length, tilt it around to mix, then pour the syrup into 4 x 200 ml (7 fl oz) metal pudding basins. Swirl the caramel over the base and sides. Leave to cool for 10 minutes.

Put the cocoa, coffee and boiling water into a mixing bowl and stir to create a smooth paste. Add the eggs, egg yolks and sugar and stir until smooth.

Pour the milk into the empty caramel pan and bring just to the boil. Gradually whisk the hot milk into the cocoa mixture, then strain through a sieve into a jug. Pour the mixture into the caramel-lined basins, cover the tops with greased foil and put the basins into the slow cooker pot. Pour enough boiling water into the slow cooker pot to come halfway up the sides of the basins, then cover with the lid and cook on low for 3–4 hours until set. Remove from the slow cooker and leave to cool, then chill in the refrigerator for 3–4 hours or overnight.

To serve, dip the basins in hot water, count to 10, then loosen the edges of the puddings with a round-bladed knife and turn out on to shallow dishes.

For vanilla crème caramels, follow the caramel recipe above and use it to line the basins. Mix 2 eggs with 3 egg yolks, 2 tablespoons caster sugar and 1 teaspoon vanilla extract. Add the hot milk and continue as above.

added
extras

duck, pork & apple rillettes

Preparation time **30 minutes**, plus chilling
Cooking temperature **high**
Cooking time **5–6 hours**
Serves **4**

2 **duck legs**
500 g (1 lb) **rindless belly pork rashers**, halved
1 **onion**, cut into wedges
1 **sharp dessert apple**, such as Granny Smith, peeled, cored and thickly sliced
2–3 **thyme sprigs**
250 ml (8 fl oz) **chicken stock**
150 ml (¼ pint) **dry cider** or **extra chicken stock**, if prreferred
salt and **pepper**

Preheat the slow cooker if necessary; see the manufacturer's instructions. Put the duck legs and belly pork rashers into the base of the slow cooker pot. Tuck the onion and apple between the pieces of meat and add the thyme sprigs.

Pour the stock and cider, if using, into a saucepan and add plenty of salt and pepper. Bring to the boil, then pour the mixture into the slow cooker pot. Cover with the lid and cook on high for 5–6 hours or until the duck and pork are cooked through and tender.

Lift the meat out of the slow cooker pot with a slotted spoon and transfer to a large plate, then leave to cool for 30 minutes. Peel away the duck skin and remove the bones. Shred the duck and pork into small pieces and discard the thyme sprigs. Scoop out the apple and onion with a slotted spoon, finely chop and mix with the meat, then taste and adjust the seasoning if necessary.

Pack the chopped meat mix into 4 individual dishes or small le parfait jars and press down firmly. Spoon over the juices from the slow cooker pot to cover and seal the meat. Leave to cool, then transfer to the refrigerator and chill well. When the fat has solidified on the top, cover each dish with a lid or clingfilm and store in the refrigerator for up to 5 days. Serve the rillettes with warm crusty bread and a few radishes, if liked.

For chicken, pork & prune rillettes, omit the duck and put 2 chicken leg joints into the slow cooker pot with the belly pork rashers, onion and thyme, replacing the apple with 75 g (3 oz) ready-to-eat pitted prunes. Continue as above.

fish terrine

Preparation time **30 minutes**, plus cooling
Cooking temperature **high**
Cooking time **3–4 hours**
Serves **6–8**

oil, for greasing
375 g (12 oz) **boneless haddock** or **cod loin**, cubed
2 **egg whites**
grated rind of ½ **lemon**
juice of 1 **lemon**
250 ml (8 fl oz) **double cream**
125 g (4 oz) **smoked salmon** or **trout**, sliced
150 g (5 oz) **salmon** or **trout fillet**, thinly sliced
salt and **pepper**

Preheat the slow cooker if necessary; see the manufacturer's instructions. Lightly oil a 1 litre (1¾ pint) soufflé dish and line the base with a circle of nonstick baking paper (check first that the dish will fit in the slow cooker pot). Blend the haddock or cod loin, egg whites, lemon rind, half the lemon juice and salt and pepper in a food processor until roughly chopped, then gradually add the cream and blend until just beginning to thicken.

Arrange half the smoked fish slices over the base of the dish. Spoon in half the fish mousse and spread it out to level off the surface. Mix the fish fillet slices with the remaining lemon juice and some pepper, then arrange on top. Top with the remaining mousse and smoked fish.

Cover the top with foil and lower the dish into the slow cooker pot. Pour enough boiling water into the pot around the dish to come halfway up the sides of the dish. Cover with the lid and cook on high for 3–4 hours or until the fish is cooked through and the terrine is set.

Lift the dish out of the slow cooker pot using oven gloves and leave to cool for 2 hours. Loosen the edge, turn out the terrine on to a plate and peel off the lining paper. Cut into thick slices. Serve with salad and toast, if liked.

For smoked haddock & chive terrine, make up the white fish mousse as above and flavour with 4 tablespoons chopped chives, 2 tablespoons chopped capers and the grated rind and juice of half a lemon. Omit the smoked fish and arrange 1 sliced tomato over the base of the dish. Cover with half the fish mousse, 150 g (5 oz) thinly sliced smoked cod fillet, then the remaining fish mousse. Continue as above.

potted pork with mustard

Preparation time **20 minutes**,
  plus cooling
Cooking temperature **high**
Cooking time **5–6 hours**
Serves **4**

650 g (1 lb 5 oz) **belly
  pork slices**
1 **onion**, chopped
3 **thyme sprigs**, plus extra
  leaves to garnish
150 ml (¼ pint) **boiling
  chicken stock**
2 teaspoons **wholegrain
  mustard**
4 tablespoons **cream sherry**
  or **extra chicken stock**,
  if preferred
salt and **pepper**

Preheat the slow cooker if necessary; see the manufacturer's instructions. Arrange the pork snugly in a tight-fitting layer over the base of the slow cooker pot. Sprinkle over the onion and add the thyme sprigs.

Mix the boiling stock with the mustard, sherry, if using, and a little salt and pepper. Pour the mixture over the pork. Cover with the lid and cook on high for 5–6 hours until the pork is very tender.

Discard the thyme sprigs, then lift out each pork slice 1 at a time on to a plate, discard the skin and fat and put the meat on a second plate. Continue until all the meat is on one plate and the trimmings are on the other plate. Shred the meat into small pieces with a knife and fork.

Strain the juices from the slow cooker pot. Pack the pork and a little of the onion into 2 wide-necked jars, moistening with a little of the strained cooking liquid. Press the pork down firmly, then spoon over the remaining cooking liquid to cover completely and sprinkle with a few extra thyme leaves. Leave to cool, then clip the lids in place and store in the refrigerator for up to 5 days. To serve remove the top layer of fat from the jars and scoop the potted pork on to warm crusty bread, if liked.

For potted pork with peppercorns, omit the wholegrain mustard and add 1 teaspoon Dijon mustard. Cook as above, then shred the pork and finely chop the prunes. Mix with 1 teaspoon roughly crushed peppercorns and 1 teaspoon drained and chopped capers, then pack into a jar with some of the strained juices and a little onion as above.

garlicky pork terrine

Preparation time **30 minutes**,
  plus overnight chilling
Cooking temperature **high**
Cooking time **5–6 hours**
Serves **6–8**

12 **smoked streaky bacon
  rashers**, about 250 g (8 oz)
  in total
 250 g (8 oz) **minced pork**
250 g (8 oz) **turkey or
  chicken breast strips**,
  chopped
150 g (5 oz) **chicken livers**,
  defrosted if frozen, any white
  cores discarded, then finely
  chopped
2 **spring onions**, finely chopped
2 **garlic cloves**, finely chopped
3 tablespoons **brandy**
50 g (2 oz) **fresh breadcrumbs**
1 **egg**, beaten
¼ teaspoon **ground cloves**
1 teaspoon coarsely crushed
  black peppercorns
175 g (6 oz) chilled carton
  chimichurri or **marinated
  pimento-stuffed green
  olives**, halved
salt

Preheat the slow cooker, if necessary; see the
manufacturer's instructions. Line the base of a 15 cm
(6 inch) diameter soufflé dish that is 8 cm (3¼ inches)
high with nonstick baking paper. Stretch a few of the
bacon rashers with the back of a knife to 1½ times as
long. Use to line the base and sides of the dish, reserving
a few to cover the top once filled. Chop the remaining
bacon and add it to a large mixing bowl with the pork,
turkey or chicken, livers, spring onions and garlic. Mix in
the brandy, if using, breadcrumbs, egg and cloves, then
season. Sprinkle the chimichurri sauce or olives over the
mixture, then gently fold together. Spoon the mixture
into the bacon-lined dish and press down well. Fold the
edges of the bacon over the top, then cover with the
remaining stretched-out bacon slices, trimming to fit.

Cover the dish with nonstick baking paper and foil
and put it into the slow cooker pot. Pour enough boiling
water into the pot to reach halfway up the sides of the
dish, then cover and cook on high for 5–6 hours until
cooked through (the blade of a small knife inserted into
the centre of the terrine and held for 10 seconds should
feel hot when removed and any juices should run clear).

Remove the dish from the slow cooker with oven gloves,
stand it on a plate and cover the top with a plate to act
as a weight. Chill overnight. To serve, uncover, run a knife
around the dish, invert the dish on to a plate, then, holding
the dish and plate, jerk to release. Peel off the paper and
scrape off any excess jelly. Cut into slices to serve.

For garlicky pork & pimento terrine, omit the olives
and add 175 g (6 oz) drained red pimento from a jar,
cut into small pieces. Continue as above.

best-ever barbecue sauce

Preparation time **15 minutes**
Cooking temperature **high**
Cooking time **5–6 hours**
Makes **about 1 kg (2 lb)**

2 **onions**, finely chopped
2 small **cooking apples**,
   450 g (14½ oz) in total,
   peeled, cored and finely
   chopped
500 g (1 lb) **passata**
4 tablespoons **dark
   muscovado sugar**
2 tablespoons **sherry vinegar**
1 tablespoon **Worcestershire
   sauce**
1 teaspoon **dry English
   mustard powder**
salt and **pepper**

Preheat the slow cooker if necessary; see the manufacturer's instructions. Add all the ingredients to the slow cooker pot. Stir together, then cover with the lid and cook on high for 5–6 hours, stirring once during cooking and again at the end.

Pour into warm, dry jars to the very top, then screw on the lids. Label and leave to cool. Store in the refrigerator for up to 1 month or pack into plastic containers and freeze for up to 3 months. Defrost in the refrigerator overnight. Serve with burgers, sausages or steak, if liked.

For Cajun sauce, add 1 teaspoon ground allspice, 1 teaspoon ground cinnamon, ½ teaspoon hot smoked paprika and 1 teaspoon crushed dried red chillies to the other barbecue sauce ingredients. Cook as above.

christmas cranberry sauce

Preparation time **10 minutes**
Cooking temperature **high**
Cooking time **3–4 hours**
Serves **10**

500 g (1 lb) **fresh cranberries**
125 g (4 oz) **caster sugar**
125 ml (4 fl oz) **ruby port** or
  fresh orange juice
juice of **1 orange**
2 teaspoons **cornflour**
  (optional)

Preheat the slow cooker if necessary; see the manufacturer's instructions. Add the cranberries to the slow cooker pot, sprinkle with the sugar, then pour over the port, if using, and orange juice.

Cover and cook on high for 3–4 hours until the cranberries are softened. Stir well, roughly crushing any large berries. If you prefer a slightly thicker sauce, mix the cornflour to a smooth paste with 1 tablespoon cold water, then stir the paste into the hot sauce, re-cover and cook for 10 minutes. Spoon into a wide-necked jar, leave to cool, then clip the jar closed. Store in the refrigerator for up to 1 week.

For gingered cranberry sauce, omit the port and add 125 ml (4 fl oz) ginger wine and 2.5 cm (1 inch) peeled and finely chopped fresh root ginger.

fiery tropical chutney

Preparation time **25 minutes**
Cooking temperature **high**
Cooking time **4–5 hours**
Makes **4 x 375 g (12 oz) jars**

250 ml (8 fl oz) **distilled
malt vinegar**
250 g (8 oz) **granulated
sugar**
2 large **red chillies**, halved,
deseeded and finely
chopped
4 cm (1½ inch) piece of **fresh
root ginger**, peeled and
finely chopped
2 teaspoons **black mustard
seeds**
1 teaspoon **cumin seeds**,
roughly crushed
1 teaspoon **coriander seeds**,
roughly crushed
½ teaspoon **turmeric**
½ teaspoon **salt**
pepper
2 large **mangoes**, peeled,
pitted and diced
1 large **pineapple**, peeled,
cored and diced
2 **onions**, finely chopped

Preheat the slow cooker if necessary; see the
manufacturer's instructions. Put the vinegar and sugar
in a saucepan and heat gently, stirring, until the sugar
has dissolved. Mix in the red chillies, ginger, seeds,
turmeric, salt and pepper.

Put the mangoes, pineapple and onions into the
slow cooker pot, pour over the hot vinegar mix, then
cover and cook on high for 4–5 hours until the fruit
is almost translucent.

Mash the fruit slightly, if liked, then ladle the chutney
into warm, dry jars to the very top, making sure there are
no air pockets. Cover with screw-on lids, label and leave
to cool. Store in a cool, dry place for up to 3 months.
Once opened, store in the refrigerator and consume
within 2 weeks.

For sweet tropical mango & pineapple chutney,
omit the chillies and continue as above.

spicy tomato 'sandwich' chutney

Preparation time **20 minutes**
Cooking temperature **high**
Cooking time **6–7 hours**
Makes **5 x 375 g (12 oz) jars**

500 g (1 lb) **cooking apples**,
  peeled, cored and diced
500 g (1 lb) **butternut
  squash**, peeled, deseeded
  and diced
500 g (1 lb) **onions**, finely
  chopped
500 g (1 lb) **tomatoes**,
  roughly chopped (no need
  to skin, unless preferred)
125 g (4 oz) **sultanas**
1 teaspoon **crushed dried
  red chillies**
1 teaspoon **ground ginger**
1 teaspoon **turmeric**
1 teaspoon **cumin seeds**,
  roughly crushed
1 teaspoon **salt**
250 g (8 oz) **light muscovado
  sugar**
250 ml (8 fl oz) **red wine
  vinegar**

Preheat the slow cooker if necessary; see the
manufacturer's instructions. Add the apples, vegetables
and sultanas to the slow cooker pot. Sprinkle over the
spices, salt and sugar and stir together.

Pour over the vinegar, cover with the lid and cook on
high for 6–7 hours, stirring the chutney once and again
at the end, until the vegetables are soft. If you prefer
a fine-textured chutney, mash the cooked chutney.

Spoon the hot chutney into warm, dry jars to the
very top and press down well, ensuring there are no air
pockets. Cover with a screw-on lid, then store in a cool,
dry place for up to 3 months. Leave the chutney to stand
for at least 2–3 days before serving so that the flavours
can mellow. Once opened, store in the refrigerator and
consume within 2 weeks. Add to cheese and salad or
ham sandwiches or try in hot toasted sandwiches, if liked.

For spicy tomato & courgette chutney, omit the
butternut squash and replace with 375 g (12 oz) diced
courgette and 1 red pepper, cored, deseeded and
diced. Continue as above.

old-fashioned lemon & lime curd

Preparation time **20 minutes**
Cooking temperature **low**
Cooking time **3–4 hours**
Makes **2 x 375 g (12 oz) jars**

125 g (4 oz) **unsalted butter**
400 g (13 oz) **caster sugar**
grated rind and juice of
  2 **lemons**
grated rind and juice of
  3 **limes**
4 **eggs**, beaten

Preheat the slow cooker if necessary; see the manufacturer's instructions. Put the butter and sugar into a saucepan, add the citrus rinds, then strain in the citrus juices. Heat gently for 2–3 minutes, stirring occasionally, until the butter has melted and the sugar has dissolved.

Pour the mixture into a basin that will fit comfortably into the slow cooker pot. Leave to cool for 10 minutes, then gradually strain in the beaten eggs and mix well.

Cover the basin with foil and place it in the slow cooker pot. Pour boiling water into the slow cooker pot around the basin so that it reaches halfway up the sides of the basin, then cover with the lid and cook on low for 3–4 hours, stirring once, until the curd is thick and falls slowly from a spoon.

Take the basin out of the slow cooker using oven gloves, stir once more, then spoon it into 2 warm, dry jars. Add a waxed paper disc to the top of each jar, then screw on the lid. Leave to cool, then store in the refrigerator for up to 3 weeks.

For orange & cranberry curd, add the butter and sugar to a saucepan. Add the grated rind of 1 orange and 2 lemons, then strain in the juice. Add the eggs, then mix in 50 g (2 oz) finely chopped dried cranberries and cook as above.

clementine marmalade

Preparation time **30 minutes**
Cooking temperature **high**
Cooking time **4–5 hours**
Make **6 x 375 g (12 oz) jars**

1 kg (2 lb) **clementines**,
   washed and quartered
1 litre (1¾ pints) **boiling water**
juice of 2 **lemons**
2 kg (4 lb) **preserving sugar**

Preheat the slow cooker if necessary; see the manufacturer's instructions. Finely chop the clementines in batches in a food processor or using a knife. Add the chopped fruit and any juices to the slow cooker pot.

Pour over the boiling water, cover with the lid and cook on high for 4–5 hours or until the fruit rinds are very soft.

Transfer the mixture to a preserving pan, add the lemon juice and sugar and heat gently, stirring from time to time, until the sugar has completely dissolved.

Bring the marmalade to the boil and boil rapidly for 15–20 minutes until a set is reached. To test, spoon a little marmalade on to a cold saucer, leave for 1–2 minutes, then run a finger through the marmalade. It should wrinkle and leave a trail where your fingertip has been.

Ladle the marmalade into warm, dry jars right to the top. Screw on the lids, label and leave to cool. Store in a cool place for up to 3 months and store in the refrigerator once opened. Consume within 2 weeks with toast, if liked.

For orange & lemon marmalade, finely chop 4 oranges and 3 lemons in place of the clementines and cook as above. Tie the pips from the fruit in a muslin bag and add to the slow cooker and later the preserving pan when cooking. Stir in the sugar, omitting the lemon juice and boil to setting point. Discard the bag of pips just before spooning into jars. Jar and store as above.

skier's hot chocolate

Preparation time **10 minutes**
Cooking temperature **low**
Cooking time **2–3 hours**
Serves **4**

100 g (3½ oz) good-quality
plain dark chocolate,
broken into pieces
25 g (1 oz) **caster sugar**
750 ml (1¼ pints) **full-fat milk**
few drops of **vanilla extract**
¼ teaspoon **ground cinnamon**
3 tablespoons **Kahlúa coffee
liqueur** (optional)
mini marshmallows, to serve

Preheat the slow cooker if necessary; see the manufacturer's instructions. Put the chocolate and sugar in the slow cooker pot, then add the milk, vanilla extract and cinnamon.

Cover with the lid and cook on low for 2–3 hours, whisking once or twice, until the chocolate has melted and the drink is hot. Stir in the Kahlúa, if using. Ladle into mugs and top with a few mini marshmallows.

For hot chocolate with brandy cream, make up the hot chocolate as above, replacing the Kahlúa with 3 tablespoons brandy, if using. Whip 125 ml (4 fl oz) double cream with 2 tablespoons icing sugar until soft peaks form, then gradually whisk in 3 tablespoons brandy, if liked. Pour the hot chocolate into mugs, then top with spoonfuls of the whipped cream and dust lightly with drinking chocolate powder or grated chocolate.

hot mexican coffee

Preparation time **10 minutes**
Cooking temperature **low**
Cooking time **2–3 hours**
Serves **4**

50 g (2 oz) **cocoa powder**
4 teaspoons **instant coffee
   granules**
1 litre (1¾ pints) **boiling water**
150 ml (¼ pint) **dark rum**
   (optional)
100 g (3½ oz) **caster sugar**
½ teaspoon **ground
   cinnamon**
1 large **dried** or **fresh red
   chilli**, halved, plus extra to
   decorate (optional)
150 ml (¼ pint) **double cream**
2 tablespoons **grated dark
   chocolate**, to decorate

Preheat the slow cooker if necessary; see the manufacturer's instructions. Put the cocoa and instant coffee in a bowl and mix to a smooth paste with a little of the boiling water.

Pour the cocoa paste into the slow cooker pot. Add the remaining boiling water, the rum, if using, sugar, cinnamon and red chilli and mix together. Cover with the lid and cook on low for 2–3 hours until piping hot or until the coffee is required.

Stir well, discard the chilli, then ladle into heatproof glasses. Whip the cream until it is just beginning to hold its shape and spoon a little into each glass. Decorate each drink with a little grated chocolate and a dried chilli, if liked.

For hot mocha coffee, reduce the amount of boiling water to 900 ml (1½ pints) and use 1 teaspoon vanilla extract instead of the rum and chilli. Cook as above, then whisk in 300 ml (½ pint) milk. Pour into heatproof glasses, top with cream as above and decorate with a few mini marshmallows.

bonfire night mulled cider

Preparation time **5 minutes**
Cooking temperature **high**
  and **low**
Cooking time **3–4 hours**
Serves **6**

1 litre (1¾ pints) **dry cider**
150 ml (¼ pint) **whisky**
1 **vanilla pod**, slit
4 cm (1½ inch) piece of **fresh
  root ginger**, peeled and
  thinly sliced
1 **cinnamon stick**, broken in 2
125 g (4 oz) **light muscovado
  sugar**
50 g (2 oz) **butter**

Preheat the slow cooker if necessary; see manufacturer's instructions. Pour the cider and whisky into the slow cooker pot. Scrape the seeds from the vanilla pod, then add these and the pod to the slow cooker pot along with the ginger, cinnamon and sugar.

Cover with the lid and cook on high for 1 hour. Reduce the heat and cook on low for 2–3 hours until piping hot. Add the butter, stir until melted, then ladle into heatproof glasses and discard the vanilla pod.

For honeyed cinnamon mulled cider, omit the vanilla and sugar and add to the slow cooker pot 4 tablespoons clear honey and the rind from 1 orange, pared off in strips, along with the squeezed juice. Continue as above.

blackberry mulled wine

Preparation time **5 minutes**
Cooking temperature **high**
  and **low**
Cooking time **3–4 hours**
Serves **6**

75 cl bottle of **red wine**
150 ml (¼ pint) **dark rum**
200 ml (7 fl oz) **orange juice**
400 ml (14 fl oz) **cold water**
150 g (5 oz) **caster sugar**
200 g (7 oz) **blackberries**
1 **cinnamon stick**, broken into
  2 pieces
1 **orange**, halved and sliced,
  to serve

Preheat the slow cooker if necessary; see the manufacturer's instructions. Pour the wine, rum, orange juice and measurement water into the slow cooker pot. Add the sugar, blackberries and cinnamon and stir together.

Cover with the lid and cook on high for 1 hour, then reduce the heat to low and continue to cook for 2–3 hours. Ladle into heatproof glasses and serve each with a half slice of orange.

For traditional mulled wine, omit the blackberries and heat the red wine, orange juice and water with sugar and 2 cinnamon sticks, adding 1 orange, cut into chunks and spiked with 4 cloves, plus a little grated nutmeg and a 2.5 cm (1 inch) piece of fresh root ginger, peeled and thinly sliced. Cook as above.

index

acknowledgements

Executive Editor Eleanor Maxfield
Senior Editor Leanne Bryan
Designer Jaz Bahra
Design and Art Direction Penny Stock
Photographer William Shaw
Home Economist Sara Lewis
Props Stylist Kim Sullivan
Production Controller Allison Gonsalves

Photography by William Shaw/Octopus Publishing Group

Additional photography:
Octopus Publishing Group Stephen Conroy 11, 27, 33,
37, 41, 63, 73, 89, 95, 103, 117, 121, 123, 147, 173,
179, 181, 207, 209, 227, 229; William Shaw 57, 91,
127, 149, 153, 201, 203.

Slow cookers kindly loaned for testing and photography
from Morphy Richards.